PATHWAYS TO
ORGANIZATIONAL WEALTH

Managers today are expected to be super-human. They must regularly balance the interests of powerful stakeholders while leading their organizations on precarious paths to wealth creation.

A big thank you to Carin Tedesco, designer of the cover art, who captured these super-human efforts in an explosive, comic book style.

PATHWAYS TO ORGANIZATIONAL WEALTH

¡POW!

DUNCAN ROBINS

To order additional copies of this book, contact:
Xlibris Corporation
1-888-795-4274
www.Xlibris.com
Orders@Xlibris.com
34265

Thank you to my family (Darcy, Day and Canyon) whose encouragement and emotional support allow me to continually pursue my intellectual curiosity.

Contents

PROLOGUE

HOW *¡POW!*, THE TOOL, CAME ABOUT

¡POW!, the tool, was crafted during actual experiences I weathered while on many successful (and painful) assignments in organizations as their leader or as a consultant. *¡POW!*, the book, is my attempt to capture and describe the management framework that I have been actively developing, testing and applying for the past three years (and one that I wish I had known many years ago).

This tool has been deceptively difficult to create. Even during periods of intense clarity, when I could visualize key parts of the framework, words escaped me. There didn't appear to be common words or phrases that could describe what was being constructed, or at least they weren't in my tool box.

My descriptive deficiencies were frustrating. My vocabulary challenges ranged from the simple to the esoteric. What should I call this thing: a tool, framework, method, approach, strategy, theory? What should I call an organization that is driven by something more than physical and social assets or constructs? How can one define value in a way that encompasses organizations of all types?

My hypotheses, flow diagrams and descriptors spanned the sociological spectrum from the physical to the spiritual, from the logical to the emotional. The organizations I have been fortunate enough to experience have also varied widely, from manufacturing companies to public benefit organizations, from web-based start-ups to faith-based initiatives, from family-owned businesses to government-funded organizations.

Fortunately, my family, friends and colleagues survived the birthing of these ideas. They laughed at the pained expressions that contorted my face during lengthy hand-waving explanations. They feigned interest as I paraded numerous charts before them. But mostly they offered suggestions and encouragement. Encouragement to keep searching, thinking, testing, contemplating . . .

Pathways to Organizational Wealth gelled in one specific moment. After several years of scratching notes on legal pads, pecking at my computer and flapping my arms, my epiphany came out of the blue, literally. I was stuffed into a seat on a commuter flight, sweating from my mad dash to meet the plane. My stomach gurgled after slamming a diet coke. I was planning to ponder the countless must-do's in my turn-around assignment when *¡POW!* It hit me. I had found the cornerstone for my construction and some important language that could cement my ideas.

This book has been created as a teaching tool. My observations, descriptions and discussions will be as brief as possible. They will be deep enough to offer subtleties, but short enough to allow for a quick read (and write!). The examples discussed are based on my personal experiences. In all cases names, places, and incidents have been disguised and quotations have been paraphrased. Why? Primarily to remove distracting information—Does it really matter what organization it was or what specific words were spoken? And secondarily, to protect those involved from the notoriety this book will give them (ha!).

For those who don't know me or my work, a warning: I am biased. I am a self proclaimed "competitive compassionate". I have a passion for building and leading successful teams and organizations. My family, friends, colleagues and those who survived my last book *"Business Euphoria—Powering Relational Organizations with Gangs, Gall and Gossip"* know that I enjoy developing and implementing winning formulas that are mechanically logical and emotionally energizing.

My bias has been shaped over time. Competition and logic dominated most of my early life. I was trained as a world-class athlete, a scientist, a financial analyst and a business consultant by arguably the best organizations in the world. More recently, compassion, creativity and patience have been added to my coaching quiver with the support of my family, by practicing organizational leadership, and through personal exploration.

This book has been fun for me to write. I hope you enjoy the read.

Note: I have included a glossary for a quick reference in the back of the book for the important terms used in my descriptions.

CHAPTER 1

WHY *¡POW!*, THE FRAMEWORK,
WAS DEVELOPED

How managers balance competing stakeholder claims on limited resources while leading and building organizations in dynamic environments has interested me for years. I've been intrigued with the very different but equally successful value-building paths taken by various types of organizations; from industrial enterprises to web-based start-ups; from advocacy groups to community hospitals. I've been fascinated by the potential impact a variation in the prioritization of stakeholders or an adjustment in the relative allocation of scarce resources can have on an organization's success. And fortunately, I've had the opportunity while on assignment (leading or consulting to a diverse group of organizations) to study the value-building paths taken by many different types of organizations.

Pathways to Organizational Wealth, (or *¡POW!*), was fashioned from my direct experiences running or consulting to a large number of organizations. As a change agent, I am often tasked with leading or coaxing changes that must build significant value in relatively short periods of time. I've distilled what I have learned from my leadership and consulting assignments in a broad range of organizations into this framework that will help managers define their primary stakeholders and more nimbly steer their organizations in the direction of health and wealth.

Important organizational patterns emerged as this new framework crystallized. This management tool became more clear and valuable after applying and refining it during a number of my assignments. Eventually, it was applicable and invaluable whether I was running a manufacturing company or consulting to a university; whether I was leading a web-based start-up towards venture financing or reengineering a for-profit education company.

I admit that I have more than just an intellectual interest in this project. My effectiveness as a leader and consultant to organizations in transition depends on making difficult decisions. I've needed this framework as a management tool in order to tackle new assignments efficiently and effectively. *¡POW!* provides me with a framework for assessing an organization and its most likely strategic options immediately—during my first hours, days and weeks on the job!

While applying the *¡POW!* framework, managers like myself will gain insight into how their organization might best prioritize multiple stakeholder demands and invest scarce resources to optimize their value-building efforts. By looking at their organization from the various perspectives of primary stakeholders managers will gain a more complete and integrated view of the possible *Pathways to Organizational Wealth*. This new management tool will also illustrate the impact on value that can be created through the reallocation of scarce resources during a progressive turn-around. And will explain the various organizational conditions that will typically arise during value creation.

Early in my career, while leading manufacturing organizations, I found the operational levers obvious and available. I could remember them as illustrated in my dusty business school texts and hear my old professors' lectures echo in my head. I understood that "profit was good" and that "shareholders rule". These golden rules, however, could only take turn-around efforts to a point well short of our organizational potential. We needed to move past our myopic focus on our shareholders and short-term profits in order to maximize our value creation. This leap seemed strangely counter intuitive to my classroom training.

Fortunately, in addition to these early manufacturing-based experiences that were dominated by powerful shareholders, I also witnessed the dramatic impact on organizational energy, momentum and value creation that could be generated by passionate tribes of employees driven by intoxicating missions. These extreme experiences had a profound impact on my current belief in and commitment to the value-creating powers of motivated employees. Enabling employees and putting them first is in vogue. It's actually very "PC" to be a leader lauding his employees. And I enjoy hearing and reading about enterprises built on the devotion and creativity of their staffs.

But why are most of these heralded, employee-driven, success stories written about service-based organizations and not equipment-dominated manufacturing enterprises like I had been leading? Why did I have to fight so hard for employees in the heat of a manufacturing turn-around when companies like Federal Express, the Salvation Army and Southwest Airlines appeared to pull off employee-inspired successes so effortlessly?

¡POW! illustrates and explains why value-building efforts in manufacturing companies, service-based enterprises and public benefit organizations each require a different managerial approach. It's typical for managers of struggling organizations of all types to be goaded into utilizing "old hat" management methods developed for the once dominant manufacturing industry. Unfortunately, these heavy-industry biased approaches are often inappropriate. It is possible to create short-term results and efficiencies in many organizations by slashing operating budgets like cutting school programs or slashing hospital expenditures. Administrations of not-for-profits can demand increased productivity and output or force a new direction on their staffs that might direct them towards a more profitable market. But upset professionals in public benefit organizations, like doctors, nurses, professors and teachers, will not maximize the potential of their organizations without their needs being addressed, no matter what the business gurus suggest.

As a consultant ready to force tough decisions to get results, it was hard for me to get my bearings outside the typical manufacturing model. Aren't "shareholders" supposed to be the most important stakeholders? Didn't we have to address the needs of our "customers"? But then again, who were our shareholders or our customers? Were they our students, our students' parents, our alumni, our donors, future employers, our community, or our taxpayers? What were we trying to create if it wasn't profit? How could we maximize our positive impact and create the most "value"?

¡POW! helps managers apply the appropriate methodology to their organization by illustrating the relationships between different management approaches for various types of organizations. There are many obvious similarities between organizations. These similarities unfortunately allow, and even compel, successful business executives to apply "cookie cutter" (but often misguided) approaches in a new type of organization based on what worked in their last company.

I cringe when I think about the missteps I took during the initial stages of some of my assignments. My head and heart were filled with preconceived, errant assumptions and misdirected passion. My mistakes were rarely about what resources were available to invest or what organizational constraints we faced. Expert staff members readily produced that information. What I had to learn was which stakeholder to take care of first. And what they expected. We needed to meet our primary stakeholder's needs by leveraging our core assets as efficiently as possible and learn how much and on what timing to invest in each of our other stakeholders. On this basic level, several different classifications of organizations became evident.

¡POW! works like a managerial "GPS" for leading dynamic organizations in a rapidly changing operating environment. Defining and highlighting an organization's primary and secondary stakeholders gives managers a more personalized roadmap to organizational wealth. Whether working with manufacturing, service-based or public benefit organizations, learning to assess stakeholder priorities and expectations will shorten your organization's road to success.

The need for new management methods for non-manufacturing oriented businesses is real and growing. This should not be surprising. Significant transitions are occurring in the Western world. Many of our value creating, for-profit assets and enterprises are becoming more "social" (i.e. more human-based) and less physical. Public benefit organizations are experiencing increased levels of scrutiny and results-oriented expectations from "baby-boomers" with an abundance of time and financial resources to "invest".

Over forty years have passed since manufacturing output peaked as a percentage of the United States' Gross Domestic Product. Since that time, Western economies and corporate responsibilities have evolved. Consumer, employee and community expectations and demands have grown, diluting the power of the once mighty manufacturing companies and their shareholders. And these significant shifts in power have rendered one-dimensional managerial approaches exemplified in the title of Dr. Friedman's famous article *"The Social Responsibility of Business is to Increase Profits"* (The New York Times Magazine, September 13, 1970) and many business text books insufficient for most modern enterprises and their management teams.

In fact, Western economies have become collectively more social (i.e. more service-oriented and people-based) and less physical. Today, many enterprises are far more than physical plants and/or financial engines with market values driven solely by short-term profits. Many have significant and growing portfolios of social assets contributing to their valuations like brands, intellectual property, relationships and other human capital that can be difficult to quantify in short-term, profit-based models.

During the past 40-years, the importance (and value) of the physical has diminished. This shift has been driven by the commoditization of products, the rise of large service-based economies, and the increasing accessibility of vast amounts of information, technology, productive resources and capital. Consumers, employees and communities have gained significant power in economic equations; and their concerns/expectations are often more advanced than their historical need for the basics. This economic shift from the physical to the social is readily apparent, yet accounting and economic measurements and management methodologies do not appear to have evolved as quickly.

Most business/economic models and valuation techniques currently in use were created during a physical era when manufacturing economies dominated the West (or were based on physical data from those times). They emphasize short-term profits, the efficient utilization of physical assets, and "objective" present value of cash flows; rather than the relevance and importance of social assets, the more "subjective" future potential of productive relationships and institutional creativity, or the more esoteric drivers found in cause-based organizations.

The current operating environment is very complex. Today's managers are often challenged with creating value for many influential stakeholders (with varying and often competing expectations and interests) in the face of increased competition with scarce resources. These managers need help!

What follows is a framework for 21st century managers. *¡POW!* works as an alternative management approach, outlining not just *Pathways to Organizational Wealth*, but also health, profitability, sustainability, growth or whatever else your stakeholders desire or require. It is a multidimensional framework that takes into consideration all types of organizations, important stakeholders and their varying needs.

CHAPTER 2

¡*POW!* BACKGROUND—
THE PURPOSE OF AN ORGANIZATION

Charting a *Pathway to Organizational Wealth* must start with finding an answer to the fundamental question: **What is the purpose of an organization?** Without understanding the purpose of an organization, managers can not chart or navigate the appropriate value-creating course for their enterprise. Without resolving what is to be created by and for whom, scarce resources can not be allocated efficiently and effectively. And yet, a sound, simple answer to this basic question eludes many modern managers. There appear to be too many organizational types with too many powerful stakeholders operating in increasingly dynamic environments for an obvious answer to be readily apparent to today's organizational leaders. That is, until ¡*POW!* was developed.

While earning my MBA at Stanford University (a fantastic experience full of interesting lectures, lively discussions, and a healthy balance of work and play) I had the opportunity to participate in a very spirited debate centered on Dr. Friedman's famous thesis regarding the primary purpose of all businesses. Despite the obvious changes occurring outside our classroom and the vocal pleas of our progressive classmates, most participants understood and embraced Friedman's suggestion that: "*The Social Responsibility of Business is to Increase Profits*". It was difficult to argue. Profits belonged to those who took the risks. Those earnings could be spent by the investors as they chose. This was an implicit condition of the free market.

*   *   *

Author's Note: I consider the term "business" to be broad, encompassing organizations of many types. I suggest that any organization that has some form of employee group that creates products or delivers services for the benefit of others while investing capital and capturing/reporting results must be considered a business. However, because the term business can have a narrow definition and/or a negative connotation in some circles, I use the terms "organization" and "enterprise" primarily in this framework.)

*   *   *

Of the many lectures, case studies and discussions I experienced during my two years at Stanford, this debate has haunted me the most. The further my assignments have taken me from classic manufacturing enterprises, the more difficulty I have had applying Friedman's proposition. The debate has continued in my head and over drinks with friends for many years . . . *What is the purpose of an organization?!*

Profit is a simple and intoxicating answer to this classic question. But it doesn't fit many of the organizations I have encountered. Is the social responsibility of a hospital, school or church to increase profits? How about a law firm or a policy-oriented think tank? Even web-based service organizations like Yahoo, Amazon and Ebay appear to have rewarded their stakeholders despite pitiful profits (relative to share prices). After many work experiences, investigations and conversations, my take on the "Friedman debate" has become clear.

> *The primary purpose of an organization is to meet or exceed the expectations of wealth or value creation of its primary stakeholders by investing in and leveraging its core assets.*

The purpose of an organization must be to maximize value or wealth creation for its primary stakeholders (however its primary stakeholders define value or wealth), and not to necessarily maximize profits. The classic response "to maximize profits" assumes: 1) that the majority of investment and risk is shouldered by shareholders that desire and benefit from increasing profits; and 2) those shareholders want to be paid that financial investment back plus a reward for taking the risk which the organization affords through apportioning a part of its profits. In many organizations, however, "customers" and/or "employees" can invest and risk as much or more than "shareholders". And these customers and/or employees may not want to earn financial rewards.

Volunteers, an example of one type workforce, aren't looking to get financially rich off their investments of time and energy. Consumers might pay a premium for a service or brand without expecting a rebate. And capital contributors (i.e. "shareholders") like donors and taxpayers might not expect to be paid back at all. In fact, the majority of stakeholders involved in public benefit organizations and not-for-profits (although interested in sustainability) are more likely to be driven to increase their organization's positive impact on the community than by the potential for increasing its financial profits.

So if an organization's primary purpose is to increase value or wealth as defined by its stakeholders, we must first consider and classify an organization's stakeholders. We (the management) must then assess their needs (for value and wealth creation) and decide how to address those needs and in what order with the limited assets at our disposal.

Developing a list of stakeholders should be relatively easy for any organizational leader. Shareholders, donors, taxpayers, banks, employees, volunteers, board members, vendors, community members, voters, constituents, customers, consumers, students, patients, parishioners, and many others would all make a list of stakeholders depending on the type of organization.

Prioritizing those *stakeholders*, however, is a difficult strategic task for management. But scarce resources can not be allocated efficiently without accomplishing this task. Business managers and theorists have believed for years that shareholders should be put at the top of the list of stakeholders. More recently, the importance of and stature of customers have increased. Much has been written in the last decade about the need for customer loyalty, the power of consumers today, and the need to put them first. Similarly, there have been an increasing number of books and articles chronicling the successes realized by employee-centric organizations. And modern managers can be further confused in their prioritization efforts by the evolving regulatory and legal environment as well as increasing community demands requiring heightened awareness of organizational impacts on communal property. So, what is a manager to do? Put everyone first? Impossible!

With a quick review of the literature, one might objectively and correctly surmise that for most organizations there are three groups of stakeholders that should be in the running for the top ranking. This shortened list is supported by my experience and my discussions with managers from a broad cross-section of organizations.

Every manager I spoke with ranked "Shareholders" (broadly defined to include all those sponsors, donors, and investors that provide financial capital to an organization) as important. "Customers" (including consumers, other businesses, and all those that benefit from the products produced or services provided by an organization) were also ranked highly by executives. This view is embodied in the often repeated phrase: "The customer is always right". "Employees" (including all people that work with the organization to create the product or deliver the service that do not belong to a vendor or one of the other stakeholder groups) were also rated tops by certain organizational leaders and thought to be important by all.

Shareholders, Customers and **Employees** can often be considered the top three stakeholders of an organization. But which of these three should be ranked first, second or third, and when? My own leadership experiences as a change agent in turn-arounds and start-ups offered excellent real-life, real-time laboratories in which to test hypothetical answers to these questions.

Start-ups and organizations undergoing a turn-around must have a well defined plan, a direct pathway to organizational health, or they fail. Turn-arounds are intensely honest times for an organization. It's obvious that something is broken and an immediate fix is needed. In start-ups, like turn-arounds, there is no room for waste, special favors, or political crap. For this reason, both of these organizational states represent interesting opportunities to understand the core workings of enterprises.

Turn-around managers and entrepreneurs must continually prioritize. During the most trying times (in extreme turn-arounds and during large growth spurts) explicit rankings of stakeholders must occur every hour of every day. Who should we pay? What can we delay? What can we pull forward? What should we cut? What can we invest in? Management in these stressed organizations must simplify operations. These organizations must focus on value-creating activities, identify and leverage core assets and address the needs of the most important stakeholders first. During these exciting times managers have to be able to say, "No matter what, take care of XXX. When we find more capital/resources we will work on YYY next."

While leading organizations through challenging episodes, I have learned what should be obvious. For some organizations the Customer is number one. In some turn-arounds, we did everything we could to retain them and/or acquire more. While treating Customers like royalty, many Employees were let go and for those who stayed, work loads increased and pay was cut. Vendors were put on payment plans and threatened with less if bankruptcy occurred. Banks were forced into forbearance periods and debt restructurings. Leases were restructured or broken. Shareholders, with little power, hung on as long as they could, but demanded little while they tried to minimize their legal exposure.

In other turn-arounds and start-ups, we needed to maintain and feed our equipment at all costs. Our equipment was our primary asset. And we needed to retain our control of it. We converted raw materials into finished goods and shipped them at discounted prices to whoever could pay. We badgered our Customers for outstanding accounts receivables. We cut unnecessary labor and stretched our vendors. It was clear that Shareholders (including banks) ruled the roost in these situations. We did what was required to meet their expectations, cover our interest payments and fulfill our lease obligations in order to alleviate their concerns and keep control of our physical assets.

Other organizations I have worked with put their Employees first, especially their powerful "knowledge workers". During difficult times the best and/or most entrepreneurial of these contributors leveraged their positions into improved compensation packages. While negotiations bent on retaining key employees went on, prices charged Customers increased, services offered to Customers were reduced, interest and dividend payments were missed (or cancelled) and non-essential equipment was removed.

The more experiences I had, the more obvious the patterns became. I honed my hypotheses and investigations as the patterns formed. And ultimately the *¡POW!* framework was developed. Three very different types of organizations emerged based on the relative rankings of the primary stakeholders and on the types of core assets each organization leveraged.

¡POW! is a management method for building and maximizing the value and wealth of organizations through optimally leveraging their core assets according to the needs/expectations of their most important stakeholders. Clearly, stakeholders are only part of the answer. To allocate scarce resources appropriately, a manager must also recognize the different types of assets available, as well as their potential.

Creating a list of potential assets or resources should be easy for managers. Assets could include various pieces of equipment, buildings, contracts, know how, customer relationships, brands, patents, vendor relationships, and many more. For our purposes, however, it is me more powerful to group these many assets or resources into three distinct types: Physical Assets, Social Assets and Causal Assets.

Physical Assets are the easiest to understand and recognize. Equipment, buildings and inventory fit easily into this category. Physical Assets have important properties that a manager must take into consideration. First, a Physical Asset depreciates even when maintained. Second, it can only be utilized in one place at one time. This explicit physical scarcity can result in an associated opportunity cost when a Physical Asset is deployed. And third, a Physical Asset must typically generate more cash (or utility) than its cost of maintenance for its value to increase (holding risk factors, return expectations and replacement costs equal).

Most *Social Assets* are as easy to identify as their Physical counterparts. However, many of us are not trained to consider a brand, the location of a building, or other such items as assets. Social Assets may also come in the forms of intellectual property like patents and trademarks or know how. Customer, vendor and community relationships are also important assets in this class. Managers must recognize that Social Assets differ substantially from Physical Assets in two important ways. First, unlike its Physical cousin, a Social Asset has the ability to appreciate when maintained. Second, a Social Asset can be leveraged in multiple ways simultaneously, it doesn't have physical limitations!

Managers should also understand that a Social Asset must increase in relevance or importance to its core stakeholders while maintaining or increasing its relative scarcity at the margin for its value to increase. There is no need for a pure Social Asset to generate positive cash flows for its value to increase. Maintenance costs can be much greater than revenue produced by a Social Asset and still its value can increase. Many investors in Social Assets speculate that these assets will appreciate (be worth more to someone else in the future) due to the subjective interests of those future potential buyers, rather than relying on current cash flows (or short-term profits) to return a positive present value.

Our third class of assets is more difficult to name and describe. I classify the group as cause-based and offer them the label of *Causal Assets*. Causal Assets can be based on such esoteric concepts as values, purpose, and/or beliefs that can have an enormous impact on organizational productivity, creativity and wealth. Causal Assets can affect a person's life and an organization's development (and valuation) profoundly without necessarily having a direct link to profitability. They can be energizing, healing, rejuvenating and abundant. Examples might include the mission or purpose of an organization, its communal values, its collective norms, philosophies and beliefs.

In summary, there are three primary stakeholders in all organizations: Shareholders, Customers and Employees. Each organization can invest in and leverage three types of assets: Physical, Social and Causal. With this background we can now classify organizations according to their most important stakeholders and their core assets. After classifying organizations, *Pathways to Organizational Wealth* become easier to understand and recognize.

*   *   *

Author's Note: Few assets could be classified as purely Physical, Social, or Causal. More often assets are a blend of two or three of these classifications and lie somewhere on a continuum between the extremes. Although most can be classified by their dominant characteristics, it is important for managers to recognize each discrete value component of their core organizational assets. For example, a piece of real estate will have a Physical value based on its construction materials, size and utility. But it might also have significant Social importance associated with its location and history. And to some, it may even have a spiritual or Causal significance.

Social and Causal Assets can also be enhanced by Physical and/or Causal/Social improvements. The value of a brand (the name of an organization) might be improved by creating a captivating logo. A brand's value might also be increased by associating it with powerful causes that resonate with core stakeholders. The cause of an organization might gain popularity with a clever slogan and messaging campaign, or by building a physical structure or endowment that grounds its mission.

*   *   *

Chapter 3

¡POW! PRIMER—CLASSIFYING
ORGANIZATIONS

As outlined in the last chapter, this management framework is built on the basic premise that:

> *The primary purpose of an organization is to meet or exceed the expectations of wealth or value creation of its primary stakeholders by investing in and leveraging its core assets.*

The model also assumes that the list of primary stakeholders in all organizations can be simplified to three groups: Shareholder, Customers and Employees. It also suggests that each organization can invest in and leverage three types of assets: Physical, Social and Causal. With this background we can now classify organizations according to their core assets and their most important stakeholders.

For this framework, I had to decide whether to classify organizations first by their most dominant assets or their top stakeholder. To keep things simple and more tangible, I have chosen to lead with asset type.

An organization will invest in those core assets that can be most efficiently leveraged to create the most wealth for its primary stakeholders. Because many operations will learn to focus their operations to optimize their efforts, one class of assets will likely dominate their core operational investments and activities. Thus, the number of organizational types could be limited to three:

1) *Physical Organizations*
2) *Social Organizations*
3) *Causal Organizations*

It also seems obvious that all three of our primary stakeholders will be important and active to varying degrees in every organization, resulting in the potential for six distinct organizational subgroups based on the ranking of each:

	First	Second	Third
1)	Shareholders;	Customers;	Employees
2)	Shareholders;	Employees;	Customers
3)	Customers;	Employees;	Shareholders
4)	Customers;	Shareholders;	Employees
5)	Employees;	Customers;	Shareholders
6)	Employees;	Shareholders;	Customers

By focusing on assets first and then stakeholders, I am able to reduce the opening number of organizational types to three and include both classification requirements (assets and stakeholders) when considering the six subgroups.

Physical Organizations have core value-creating mechanisms dominated by Physical Assets. These organizations will typically require significant amounts of capital to fund their initial investments in buildings, equipment and inventory. Ongoing maintenance of these core assets will require significant reinvestments. Examples of Physical Organizations include manufacturing enterprises of all types and many distribution operations.

Manufacturing enterprises have a hunger for capital that is rarely satiated. Due to huge capital requirements and the delayed return on this type of investment, Shareholders as a class have a large amount of power. The typical goal of these Physical Organizations is to maximize the return (profits and cash generated) from these investments for their Shareholders. Reducing costs and increasing throughputs are key business drivers.

Pure manufacturing entities (i.e. very Physical, not Social or Causal) will have no brand and little technology to enhance their product offerings. These pure manufacturers are often companies that offer commodity products to their customers at market clearing prices (i.e. low). Customers have power when supply is abundant but not when supply is tight. So, manufacturers flex their throughputs in the short-term and capacities in the long-term in an effort to maximize their profitability (and minimize their Customers' power). By balancing the economic benefits of throughput with the pricing power derived from marginal scarcity, it is hoped that manufacturing activities continually produce a positive economic contribution (and profits most of the time). Employees have the lowest ranking in these organizations. Factories typically simplify and standardize the contributions of their workforce to allow for maximum flexibility (which includes "flexing" their workforces as needed).

Social Organizations are dominated by Social Assets. The core assets invested in and leveraged by Social Organizations include Customer relationships and intellectual property like brands, trademarks, and patents. In contrast with Physical Organizations, very Social enterprises have (and need) a relatively small amount of fixed overhead (i.e. Physical constructs). As a result, Social Organizations tend to be very scaleable. They have a relatively low need for initial and ongoing capital but have high current expenses like wages and advertising.

Service-based enterprises are classic Social Organizations. These organizations are driven to create value in the eyes of their Customers. Through building and protecting their coveted market shares and popular images, Social Organizations can charge premium prices, reinvest the resulting profits in their Social Assets, and build organizational wealth and value. Because service is so important, Employees are often highly respected in these organizations. Wages and bonuses are often high for their expert staffs. Shareholders must listen to the needs of the Customers and often their star contributors in order to maximize their returns. Advertising agencies, consultancies and legal practices are all examples of Social Organizations that often put their Customers first.

Causal Organizations are dominated by the communal will of their Employees—Their desire to help, to do good, and to better the world. A cause dominates the workings of these organizations. They are driven to make the world a better place by feeding, healing or counseling their Customers. Employees create the most value in these organizations and often invest the most in them. Employees typically invest far more time and energy in these organizations relative to their compensation compared with like Employees in Social Organizations. At the extreme, volunteers can make up a major part of the workforce and be paid "nothing". Many service-based, Causal Organizations require little capital. Customers are abundant and in real need. So, Employees should rank at the top of the three primary stakeholders. Capital contributors will be slightly lower on the list depending on the amount of capital required to fund the operation.

Causal Organizations can include everything from legal and advisory services (for the disadvantaged) to schools, hospitals and church organizations. The majority of Causal Organizations fall in the public benefit or not-for-profit categories as they are typically driven by something other than profits. (*Note:* "Not-for-profit" is a tax designation and not necessarily a badge indicating a cause-dominated organization. Not all not-for-profit organizations are cause-dominated, with Employees ranked top. Some might be classified as service-based organizations and place Customers first.)

In summary, this model recognizes three types of organization based on the dominant type of core assets leveraged to meet or exceed the expectations of the primary stakeholders. In my descriptions, the following pattern was suggested:

Organization Type:	Core Asset:	Primary Stakeholder:
1) Physical	Physical	Shareholders
2) Social	Social	Customers
3) Causal	Causal	Employees

This is the first step in my classification scheme for organizations. As you might have noticed in the above discussion, I was comfortable outlining who each of the dominant stakeholders should be by organizational type, but attempted to be vague in my ranking of the remaining two. To allow for the full number of possible pathways to organizational wealth, we must refine our groupings further.

Each type of organization described above must be further split into two subgroups, one for each possible ranking of the second and third stakeholders. So, Physical Organizations will always have Shareholders first, but one subgroup (Physical—Social) will place Customers second and Employees third. The second subgroup (Physical—Causal) will rank Employees second and Customers third. The complete classification system is as follows:

	Stakeholder Ranking		
Organizational Type	First	Second	Third
Physical—Social	Shareholders	Customers	Employees
Physical—Causal	Shareholders	Employees	Customers
Social—Causal	Customers	Employees	Shareholders
Social—Physical	Customers	Shareholders	Employees
Causal—Social	Employees	Customers	Shareholders
Causal—Physical	Employees	Shareholders	Customers

As described prior, commodity-oriented manufacturing businesses are solidly grounded in the set of *Physical Organizations*. However, most Physical Organizations will invest in some Social Assets and are likely to have Employees that understand the purpose of the company.

Brands and Customer relationships are typical value-added assets that enhance organizational wealth creation in Physical Organizations. Examples of *Physical—Social* organizations that are based on manufacturing commodity products with strong brands and that develop coveted relationships with their Customers (i.e. retailers) include classic consumer product companies like Procter & Gamble and General Foods. These companies fight for market share with like vendors and invest huge dollars into their production facilities, trade-related incentives and consumer-oriented, advertising campaigns and promotions. Shareholders and their expectations dominate these companies. However, with the consolidation of retailers, the might of Customers is growing. Although Employees in these organizations may be well paid, they are the least powerful primary stakeholder.

A *Physical—Causal* organization is a slight twist on the Physical type of enterprise. Shareholders concerns and expectations still dominate the workings of these companies. However, in these organizations Employees (on average) are treated much better than in there Physical—Social cousins. There is a cause that drives these organizations, but they are Physical entities first and foremost. These manufactures differentiate themselves through technical capabilities, research and development. Such organizations populate the technology sectors. Examples include bio-tech firms like Genentech, bio-medical enterprises like Medtronic and niche pharmaceutical companies.

Social Organizations are Customer-leaning. Market and mind share is critical to these businesses. Being known as the undisputed best at what they do in their market should be a primary goal. The best way to drive value and increase cash flow is to retain current Customers while gaining new ones. The most effective and efficient way to win market share for Social organizations is through word-of-mouth referrals. To get the referrals and win loyalty, these firms must meet or exceed the expectations of their Customers regularly.

For *Social—Causal* organizations, to become the best (and create the most value), Employees must be driven by that goal. These are service-based Social Organizations. They have very few Physical Assets, and little need for long-term capital. Examples include advertising and consulting agencies, law and accounting firms. Good firms know that "the customer is always right". Understandably, Customers are often very loyal to their "stars" (agency Employees). As a result, star Employees are treated very well in order to retain them (and their loyal account bases).

Social—Physical organizations invest in Physical Assets before Employees in an attempt to meet the needs of their Customers. Product-based retailers are classic examples of this type of organization. Physical stores are built and inventory is purchased in the hopes of attracting their prized Customers. Discount retailers like the "marts", drug stores, and super markets will invest heavily in Physical Assets and lay out their stores in a way that will promote and support as much self-help as possible. Employees are definitely lowest on the totem pole in these organizations. Even high-end retailers like Nordstrom or smaller boutiques that have a more obvious service-based model still provide relatively low wages to their larger staffs (augmented in some retailers with a commission opportunity).

Causal Organizations are driven by Employees that want to change the world. These organizations thrive when their missions align perfectly with the will of their collective labor pool. Those Causal Organizations that create the most value for their stakeholders are extremely passionate, resourceful, efficient and productive. They can make real differences in the world. They feed, heal, and improve the lives of those they touch.

Causal—Social organizations are easily spotted. Many are non-profits that are service-based. These enterprises create most of their value through the efforts of their staffs (Employees) which take the needs of their Customers very seriously. Examples of this type of organization include social service organizations that counsel, mentor, tutor and provide other expert advice and help through human-powered programs. These programs tend to be tailored to the needs of Customers in a particular segment of society and/or located in a particular region. Capital requirements are low and funding sources will often support the will and determination of management and their army of helpers.

Many of us will benefit from *Causal—Physical* organizations numerous times during our life times. They will bring many of us into the world, help us develop, and give us direction and hope. These organizations include many of our public benefit organizations that require large capital investments and skilled, specialized staff. These organizations include taxpayer-funded hospitals, schools, law enforcement, emergency services, our court systems and the military. All of these organizations require massive public investments in the staffs that run them and the Physical Assets that they manage for our benefit.

Each of these six organizational types has distinct aspects that differentiate it from the other five. These differing characteristics are rooted in the different core assets deployed and in the various rankings of primary stakeholders. These characteristics, in my experience and in the this theoretical model, suggest the existence of and need for six different paths of development (or *¡POW!*s), one for each of the organizational types. I will describe each of these six *Pathways to Organizational Wealth* in the following chapters, beginning with a basic outline of how I visualize these developmental paths.

Note: Summary of Organizational Classifications—Examples:

Organizational Type	General Example	Specific Examples
Physical—Social	Manufacturer-Consumer Products	Procter & Gamble
Physical—Causal	Manufacturer-Technology	Genentech, Medtronic
Social—Causal	Consulting Services	Ad Agency, Law Firm
Social—Physical	Product Retailers	Nordstrom, Sears
Causal—Social	Not-for-Profit Services	Big Brother/ Big Sister
Causal—Physical	Public Benefit Organizations	Hospitals, Universities

Chapter 4

¡POW! PRIMER—CHARTING BASICS

We, the managers of organizations, have a difficult job. We're expected to leverage the core assets of our enterprises in ways that increase our organizational wealth as defined by our primary stakeholders. Unfortunately, assets at our disposal are typically scarce. We are forced to deploy limited resources in a measured way while attempting to meet the needs of our most important stakeholders. As we begin to build organizational wealth by leveraging, allocating and reinvesting in our core assets, patterns in our operational decision-making are formed. These patterns can be depicted on a chart that will be described in this chapter.

When I began conceptually charting my work experiences, my desire was to capture and illustrate on paper those organizational behaviors that were becoming predictable. My goal was to create a visual tool that could improve managerial decision-making related to the allocation of scarce resources across numerous and often contending stakeholder interests. In the beginning, I did not have clearly defined parameters and none of the available data seemed to be appropriate for charting.

The factors I wanted to relate and compare were too different and/or too esoteric to analyze in a rigorous sense with available methods.

Through experimentation, I developed a comparative framework and refined conceptual units of measure. Soon, six distinct *Pathways to Organizational Wealth* (or *¡POW!*s) emerged: One predictable path existing for each of the six organizational subgroups: Physical—Social, Physical—Causal, Social—Causal, Social—Physical, Causal—Social, and Causal—Physical. I applied this basic model to a variety of organizations and improved on it. Soon it was ready to test on a broader collection of enterprises and now I am sharing it with you.

Fig. 1 The Chart

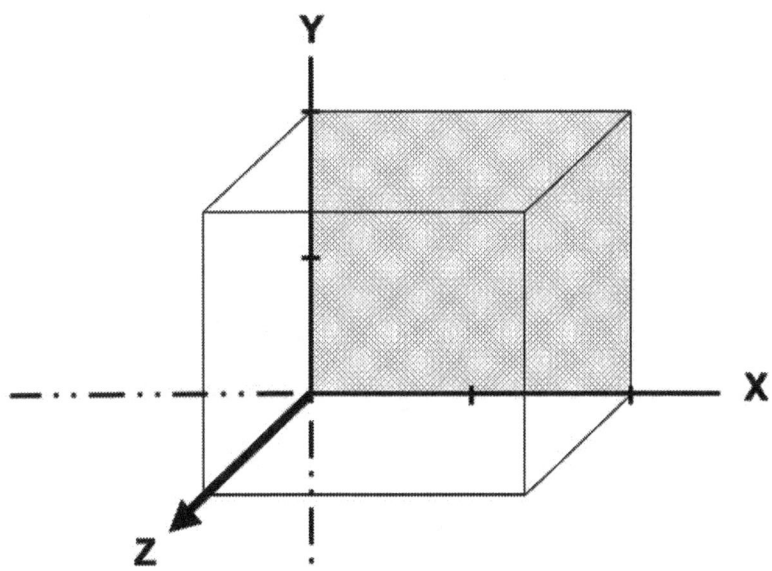

The Chart, as depicted in Figure 1, is at the heart of the visual depiction of the pathways. It can be described, in its simplest form, as a three-dimensional graph with perpendicular (or orthogonal) X, Y and Z-axes. Unfortunately, many of us find it difficult to "see" in three dimensions, so Figure 1 illustrates this concept by reproducing the chart as part of a box. To construct this in real life, draw a straight, horizontal line on a page. This will represent the X-axis. Draw another straight line vertically on the page (Y-axis) such that this second line crosses (or intersects) the first line (the X-axis) at a 90-degree angle. You should now see a perfect cross. Take your pen (Z-axis) and poke a hole into the paper right where the other two lines/axes cross such that your pen is perpendicular to the flat page (i.e. it is poking straight out at you!). Congratulations, you have now created our basic chart. To depict this construct on a flat piece of paper (so that readers don't get poked by a protruding axis!) the Z-axis is drawn at an angle as shown in Figure 1.

The *three axes* of the chart measure stakeholders' attitudes relative to their experiences with their respective organizations. I contend that the purpose of all organizations is to meet or exceed the expectations of their primary stakeholders relative to their wealth and value-building objectives. It follows that all managers need to understand how well their organizations are performing relative to primary stakeholders' expectations because stakeholders invest with the expectation that value will be created. Do the stakeholders like what they are experiencing? Or do we need to direct more of our scarce resources towards their needs? Are they content enough that we can now redirect some of our resources to the needs of other stakeholders?

The *X-Axis* measures and represents the collective opinion of Shareholders regarding the value created by an organization relative to their expectations. The *Y-Axis* measures and represents the collective opinion of Customers regarding the value created by an organization relative to their expectations. And the *Z-Axis* measures and represents the collective opinion of Employees regarding the value created by an organization relative to their expectations.

During my assignments as a turn-around manager, change agent, start-up leader and entrepreneur, I have had to understand stakeholders' needs very quickly. The first question I typically ask of stakeholders is: *What do you expect (need)?* I want to understand how they quantify those expectations and needs so that I can simplify our measurements and data collection. Fortunately, needs of each stakeholder group are surprisingly easy to collect and measure. I know what financial characteristics my Shareholders expect. I can discern the price and product or service aspects that Customers demand. And I can establish the needs of Employees. But I wanted to take this process one step further—To chart the information and compare it in a meaningful way over time.

I would expect Shareholders to be displeased if a management team set expectations that certain financial and/or operating levels would be reached by their organization and those goals were missed by a significant margin. If a product wore out faster than a Customer expected, I would expect the Customer to be upset. If an Employee received less compensation than anticipated, I would expect them to be miffed. This basic understanding compels me to regularly ask each of our stakeholders a second question: ***How well is the organization performing relative to your expectations?***

Many managers make the initial assessments regularly. However, by charting the answers to the second questions over time they will get a better understanding of how their organizations are progressing along their chosen developmental pathways, or *¡POW!*s. By understanding the six possible paths, a manager will be able to understand how best to maximize the returns from resource allocations at a strategic level according to the expectations of the primary stakeholders. Consultants and managers (like me) that regularly change industries or organizational types will more quickly synch with their new organizations' stakeholders. Business executives that join boards of non-profits will more readily affect positive change. And business students will have interesting debates for years to come!

For this chart to be a powerful managerial tool, each of the three axes should to utilize the same ***units of measure***. The units should be common to all three stakeholder groups and be as meaningful when describing the developmental paths of very Physical entities as they would be in more esoteric Causal organizations. The units of measure can't be affected by the size of an organization. And they have to be tangible and by definition, measurable.

The chart illustrates feedback from primary stakeholders based on their expectations. Each axis of the chart is split by five points equally spaced along its length. Describing the X-axis first for simplicity (as illustrated in Figure 2), the point furthest to the right represents the most positive assessment Shareholders could give their organization: *Exceeds* expectations. Less positive assessments would be *Meets* expectations and *Neither*, meaning the organization neither meets their expectations nor disappoints them. *Neither* is placed at the zero location on the X-axis. *Neither* does not register a positive nor a negative value relative to expectations. However, everything to the left of zero reflects negatively on the organization. Shareholders might answer that the organization *Disappoints* them, or outright *Upsets* them (the worst grade possible). Obviously, most executives are driven to build the value of their organizations for their stakeholders and thus desire positive rather than negative feedback. (*Note:* These same demarcations are located on the Y-axis to measure the opinions of Customers and the Z-axis to capture the thoughts of Employees. Exceeds Expectations and other positive attitudes of Customers will be located on that portion of the Y-axis above the X-axis. Positive opinions of Employees will be represented on the portion of the Z-axis that protrudes out of the page. Negative grades of Customers or Employees will be represented on the opposite sections of the relevant axes.)

What do these grades mean? On the face of it, exactly what was stated by the stakeholder: A primary stakeholder is either ecstatic with, or troubled by, your organization's efforts. To bring this closer to the operating world, a bridge can be formed from these remarks to actual operating results by creating objective, measurable goals and charting the reactions of stakeholders when results exceed or fall short of their expectations. For Shareholders, financial returns on their capital investments might be their primary concern. The X-axis could easily be calibrated to actual results by overlaying objective financial goals with likely (or actual) feedback from Shareholders. For example, as suggested in Figure 2, Shareholders would likely jump for joy if you created a cash cow (however that might be defined in numbers). They might be really Upset if you ran the company into the ground and required more financial capital. The actual numbers will depend on the organization, but expectations-based feedback from stakeholders will be universal and chartable.

Fig. 2   The Chart with Units of Measure for X-axis

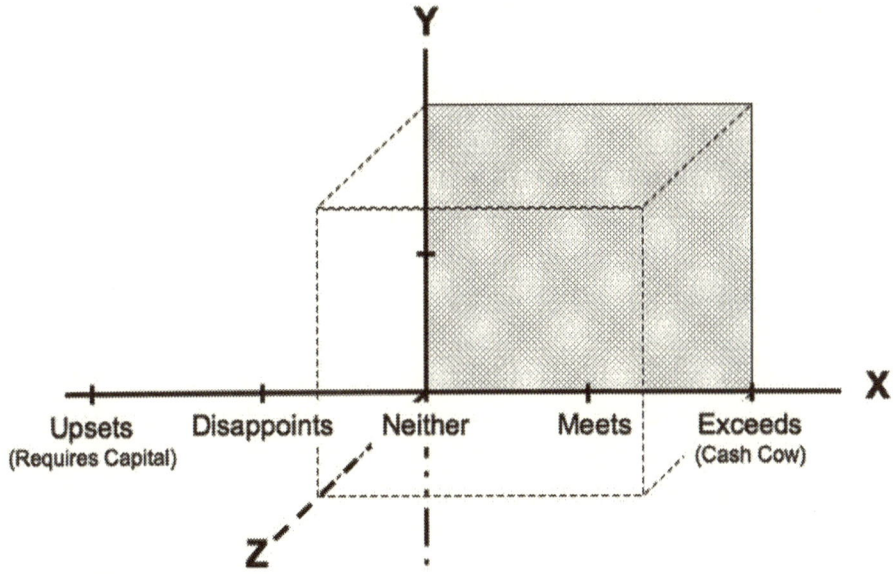

This is obviously an ***expectations-based*** management method. This approach should be intuitive to managers that understand the importance of setting achievable budgets and the gaming that is involved. This type of signaling is also prevalent between executive teams and the securities markets. For we all know the importance of beating expectations. Momentum (and significant value) is created by satiating current stakeholders and attracting more. Contented stakeholders will remain loyal, may invest more and typically allow management wider berths to operate, allocate and build. Consistently, meeting or exceeding expectations attracts additional stakeholders and the resources they are willing to invest. All this positive interest puts wind in an organization's sails which drives up its value. Unfortunately, the opposite is also true. *So, managers following this expectations-based philosophy must:*

a) understand how to set and influence the expectations of the most important stakeholders;
b) recognize where their key expectation thresholds lie; and,
c) develop a cost/benefit understanding for each grade level of each stakeholder.

Expectations of Shareholders are relatively easy to understand, measure and analyze. Many of us are well practiced in recording, producing, finding, analyzing and responding to important Physical measures that have been developed over the last 100+ years to assess the health and value of very Physical businesses. This set of data includes a large set of financial statistics (e.g. sales, gross and operating margins, cash flow) and operating information (e.g. capacity or band width, capacity utilization, though put, efficiency, quality). Investors might vary in their expectations of a company at any given point in time (e.g. how much of a reward/profit is expected for the associated risk). However, in efficient markets, there is likely to be a good understanding of the band of reasonable investor expectations for a company of a certain size, age, product/service and/or market.

This "understanding" of Physical entities and Shareholder expectations has been created and improved over the last hundred years. Language, measures and methods for quantifying Social and Causal Assets and Organizations are not as well developed. Current tools and benchmarks still favor those created for manufacturing enterprises. This shortfall is understandable. Many of us have not had the need until more recently to recognize value and wealth creation in additional, comparable ways. But our needs as managers are growing, which is why this model was created.

The X-axis measures Shareholders sentiment relative to the ability of the company to convert scarce resources into acceptable returns. The Y—and Z-axes represent the same for Social and Causal stakeholders

(Customers and Employees expectations respectively). However, overlapping measurable Social and Causal results with their expectations is more difficult. The key is in defining meaningful, quantifiable measures that represent the value that is to be created. If Customers want quality or convenience this should be easy. But how would you quantify the coolness of a brand? Perhaps by surveying the markets and registering movements in market share, pricing and sightings?

Causal needs and results might be represented by the productivity of the organization. How many people have been fed, clothed, taught? These organizations might also track the success of their students, patients, clients, and/or communities. Causal Organizations, like Social and Physical Organizations, can benefit from creating measurable goals and tracking their progress towards them provided these activities energize rather than frustrate their staffs.

*　　*　　*

Author's Note: Although it is helpful and powerful to calibrate the expectations-based measurements with actual results, this step is not necessary. This expectations-based approach does not require an objective calculation of value, or a value judgment that compares Causal Assets with Social or Physical ones. This model leaves wealth and value in the subjective minds of stakeholders which makes the model more universal.

However, by calibrating measurable operating data (like profits, quality measurements and salaries) with stakeholder expectations (first set of questions) and by comparing actual results with stakeholder feedback (second set of questions), a manager (like me or you) could link this model to operational and investment decision-making focused on delivering meaningful value-creation to stakeholders. A manager could even compare the amount of additional resources (or time) required to improve one grade level (e.g. moving from Meets to Exceeds) for each stakeholder.

*　　*　　*

After **plotting** a few organizations on the chart, it should become obvious that each of the three primary organizational types will tend to bunch around one of the three axes. Because organizations are grouped according to their core value-creating assets and the ranking of their stakeholders, these axes help describe the relative nature of organizations. Imagine an extremely Physical Organization, one that is dominated by its Physical Assets, that ranks Shareholders first amongst its stakeholders, and that is neutral relative to its Customers and Employees. (By neutral relative to its Customers and Employees I mean that this organization is only doing enough to be tolerated by these other stakeholders—They are neither happy nor upset.) This very Physical Organization would likely be plotted somewhere on or near the *X-Axis*, or the Physical Axis. Very Social or Causal Organizations will be charted near the *Y-axis* (the Social Axis) or *Z-axis* (the Causal Axis) accordingly.

For example, a manufacturer that has very powerful Shareholders, but no significant Social Assets or Employee programs of any consequence (either positive or negative), would likely be plotted on or near the X-axis. A web-based service organization that has relatively low capital needs and few Employees would be plotted on or near the Y-axis. And an organization of social activists with no paying Customers and minimal capital requirements could be spotted on or near the Z-axis.

After plotting a few more organizations on the chart, it will become obvious that there are good locations to place your organization and areas that reflect periods of difficulty. The goal is to meet or exceed the needs of all stakeholders. When an organization achieves this state, it will be located in the upper right corner of the chart (and be creating a lot of value as defined by its primary stakeholders). A struggling organization, conversely, will likely receive negative grades from stakeholders and be found outside of the box, towards the lower left of the chart (and may be destroying value).

In fact, there exist a number of interesting **zones** located on the chart as exhibited in Figure 3. In this illustration, the two dimensional X-Y section of the chart is depicted to reduce confusion. However, it should be understood that this is a three-dimensional model and these zones actually exist in three-dimensions. The chart (in this simplified 2-dimensional illustration) has been sliced into four primary zones (**I, II, III,** and **IV**) and several large regions marked as either *Unacceptable* or *Not Tolerable*. These zones and regions designate the state of an organization relative to its core stakeholders' expectations.

The *Unacceptable* region is recognizable as the most negative area, the section below the X-axis and to the left of the Y-axis. In this model, it is assumed that any organization that is Disappointing or Upsetting all of its primary stakeholders, by losing lots of money and being socially irresponsible, would be considered Unacceptable and would be terminated, or radically altered immediately.

Fig. 3   The Chart with Zones of Performance

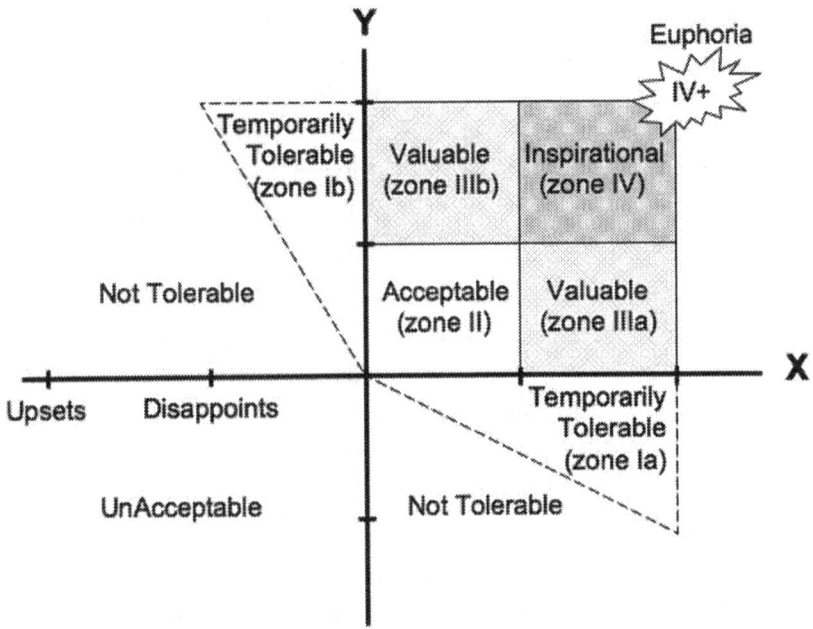

47

An organization that Upsets or Disappoints most of its stakeholders, while still managing to appease its primary stakeholder would *Not* be *Tolerable* for long. This is only slightly better than an UnAcceptable rating. A Social Organization losing a lot of money (and unsustainable) despite being socially adept, or a Physical Organization that is somewhat profitable but socially inept, would be expected to improve significantly, and as soon as possible. Angry stakeholders regardless of their ranking would demand or force action.

The dashed, diagonal lines help to outline the triangular *Temporarily Acceptable* zones Ia and Ib (and Ic in three dimensions). These areas represent (Ia) temporary stakeholder tolerance for some Social shortfalls by a Physical Organization that is on the road to profitability; or for some (temporary) financial short-falls experienced by a Social Organization (Ib) that is developing a service and/or customer-base; or small budget overages announced by a hard charging Causal Organization (Ic not pictured). Stakeholders accept the slight deviation into negative territory because the primary stakeholder is positive, the other stakeholders are only mildly Disappointed and the situation is expected to improve within an acceptable time frame.

Zone II, *Acceptable*, immediately above the X-axis and just to the right of the Y-axis (and/or Z-axis), is Acceptable to all stakeholders. This is positive territory! Stakeholders feel better than neutral about results, but they are not content. No stakeholder believes the organization is meeting their needs. As a result, operating in this positive position is rarely sustainable. Those organizations that fall into this region are attempting to please two (or three) distinctly different stakeholders, but not impressing either (any). These organizations will build little equity/loyalty with either (any) stakeholder. Their positions, as a result, will be unstable and difficult to maintain.

A *Valuable* zone (III) is a common goal for all Organizations. In a Valuable position, organizations are meeting or exceeding the expectations of their primary stakeholder and receiving positive feedback from at least its secondary stakeholder. Zone IIIa, as illustrated in Figure 3, is a common goal for many branded, consumer products companies. The investors in these Physical Organizations push for financial returns. Management invests in equipment to drive down costs and increase profits, but they also invest scarce resources into Customer-oriented assets. By building a brand, a strong market share, and loyalty, these enterprises establish a degree of pricing power and build additional organizational wealth.

Zone IIIb is a common and Valuable goal for many service-oriented organizations. These corporations strive to be known as the best-in-class for their services in their target markets and have built significant mindshare and large banks of Customer loyalty. By becoming profitable, these organizations can sustain and prosper by funding their own growth and building investor interest/confidence. As these Social Organizations build sustainable profits and tangible assets, they reduce the perception of risk and become more appealing to a broader group of investors which builds organizational value.

A Causal Organization operating in Zone IIIc (not illustrated) would have created significant value. Their primary stakeholders (Employees) will be extremely driven and a secondary stakeholder group like donors (Shareholders) would be energized. Important stakeholders would be pleased by a Causal organization that repeatedly beats operating goals while remaining within budgetary constraints. The addition or creation of a Physical construct like an endowment or building might increase the perceived viability of the organization and raise its value to potential Employees, donors and Customers.

The ultimate goal of all inspired organizations should be to exceed the expectations of their primary stakeholders while meeting the expectations of their other stakeholders, and operate in the *Inspirational* (Zone IV). However, once in a blue moon organizations exceed the needs of all stakeholders and operate in the state of *Euphoria* (Zone IV+). As I described in my book, *Business Euphoria*, this state is wonderful for all involved. Organizations operating at the apex of the chart (far upper right hand corner) are pursuing a meaningful cause and making significant social investments while building a financial engine. These euphoric organizations operate in a state that is truly abundant, energizing and extremely valuable.

Plotting the course of your organization is relatively straight forward. With the information gained from surveys, conversations and other data gathering interactions, a manager should be able to plot the location of an organization on the chart at a particular point in time. Based on the location of the organization relative to the zones described, certain concerns or considerations will be obvious. After numerous plots are made over time, management will be able to assess their organization's development relative to the expectations of its core stakeholders. Comparing the path created by drawing a line between the different plot locations (on the chart) of their organization to a typical path for a similar organization, management will be able to make further inferences. In the next few chapters, I will be describing those reference paths (or *¡POW!*s) for the six organizational types we have outlined.

CHAPTER 5

SIX PATHWAYS TO
ORGANIZATIONAL WEALTH

The goal of every organization is to meet or exceed the expectations of its primary stakeholders by leveraging its core assets. By building an enterprise that meets or exceeds expectations, management will increase the value or wealth of the organization as defined by its stakeholders. On the chart, an enterprise that is operating to the satisfaction or excitement of its stakeholders will be plotted in Zone IV and be considered Inspirational (and very valuable).

To reach the Inspirational Zone (IV), most organizations will travel through several of the other, less positive and even negative zones. A successful executive team will manage the expectations of their stakeholders while driving their organization to continually improve on their results relative to those expectations. All things being equal, well managed organizations will travel predictable paths that can be illustrated on the chart. As they build organizational wealth, these organizations will also increase the size of the positive box (square in two dimensions, cube in three dimensions created by drawing straight, perpendicular lines from the plotted position back to the related axes) exhibited on the chart in Figure 4. The growth of the box depicted on the chart reflects an enterprise that is building value by improving its results relative to the expectations of its stakeholders. The organization depicted in Figure 4, however, has not reached the state Euphoria (as indicated by the star burst in the upper right corner of the cube in the third dimension).

Fig. 4 Building Organizational Wealth (Growing the Box)

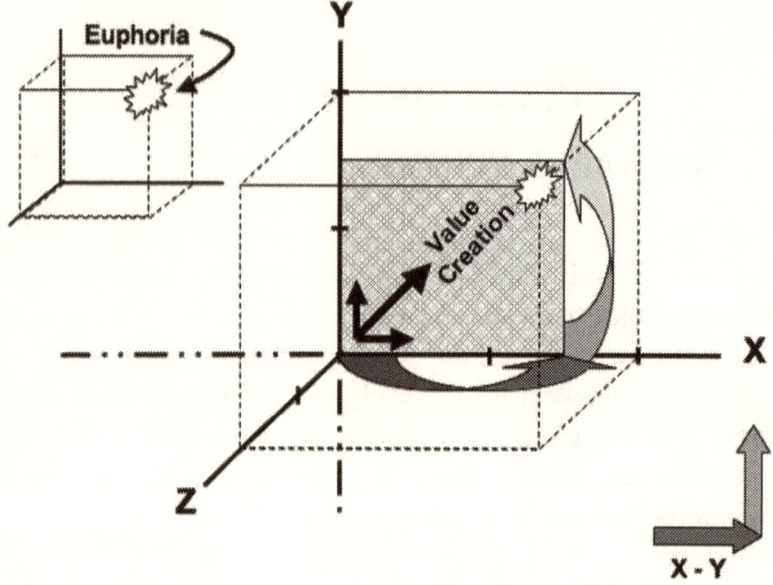

Physical ¡POW!s

Physical entities will typically first travel along the X-axis as the organization works to meet the expectations of its primary stakeholder: Shareholders. Assuming that all organizations start in a neutral position relative to all of their stakeholders (i.e. at the point where all axes cross) then the first stage of a developing Physical organization will involve traveling from this neutral position along the X-axis in a positive direction (to the right) with the goal of meeting the expectations of Shareholders.

Unfortunately, driving to the right in a consistent trajectory can be difficult with limited resources. To leverage scarce assets in a manner that will meet their primary stakeholder's needs, a developing organization will often have to "cheat" its other stakeholders for a period of time. Done delicately, and with the appropriate communication, management can direct critical resources to the needs of Shareholders with only mildly Disappointing Customers and/or Employees. With the expectation that this will be a short-lived situation, the enterprise would be plotted at position 2, and be Temporarily Tolerable (Zone I).

Management must move out of Zone I within an acceptable time period. To fund this transition, some amount of resources will have to be redirected towards the needs of Customers or Employees. This redirection of scarce resources requires the organization to ***turn-the-corner***, a more difficult maneuver for managers. During this transition, management must move away from a primarily uni-dimensional approach to asset allocation and begin the more difficult task of trading-off significant investments in at least two directions. Turning-the-corner requires disciplined managers to set the expectations of Shareholders first. These primary stakeholders must understand that continually delivering increasing profits (for instance) at the expense of all other stakeholders will not maximize value. Eventually those other stakeholders will demand attention. By winning Shareholder support for the transition, the organization will be able to turn-the-corner as illustrated in Figure 5 and begin building significant value by investing additional resources in Customers or Employees as illustrated by the increasing size of box.

Fig. 5 Turning-the-Corner

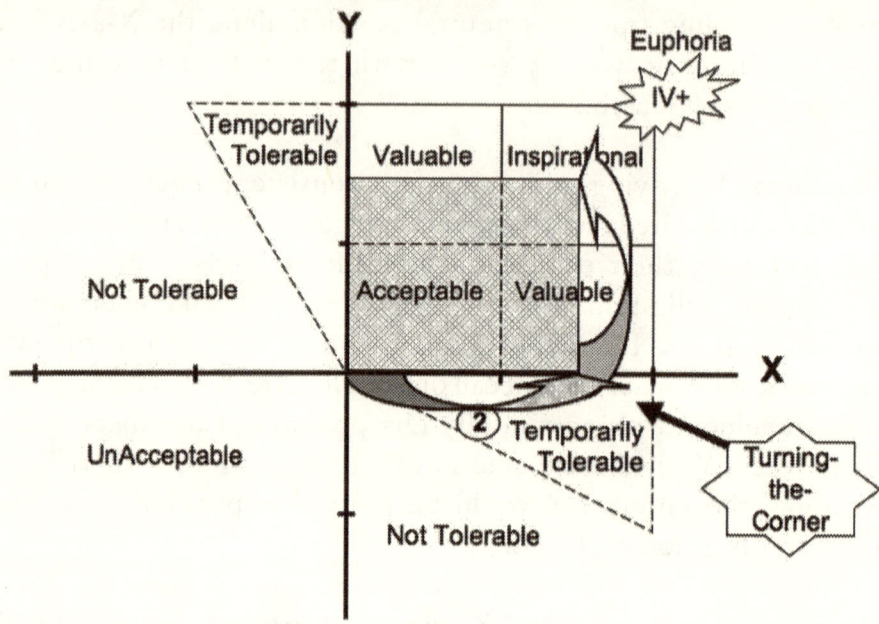

Physical—Social organizations should travel on a pathway similar to the one illustrated in Figure 5. These organizations rank their three stakeholders in the following order: Shareholders first, Customers second, and Employees third. Enterprises that are dominated by Physical Assets typically take this pathway to organizational wealth. Many manufacturing enterprises are obvious examples of organizations that fall into this group.

As manufacturing organizations grow, large amounts of financial capital are needed to build the Physical Assets required to generate wealth. Shareholders expect financial returns and rewards for the use of their capital. They may allow some financial losses initially, and set their expectations accordingly, but ultimately their needs will grow. And management will work hard to meet their expectations.

Eventually, if market conditions were as forecasted, the manufacturing plant should be able to produce enough products and sell them at prices that will allow it to meet the needs of its Shareholders. However, to maximize wealth, the management may not want to methodically fill its capacity at market prices and to the detriment of other stakeholders. The organization will need to turn-the-corner.

Turning-the-corner can be achieved by redirecting some efforts into Social Assets. By investing in Customer relationships, brands, or technology for instance, an organization should be able to build and leverage Social Assets that will interest its second most important stakeholder. These Social investments should differentiate the manufacture's operation and/or its products from rivals. If done correctly, the investments will eventually meet the needs of Customers.

Customers that are satisfied will be loyal. They will market the benefits of the organization and its products and be willing to pay a premium over market clearing prices for the manufacturer's products. With increasing demand and higher prices the organization should increase in value. If the organization manages to keep Shareholder and Customer expectations reasonable and thus not pass on all of its gains immediately to these stakeholders in the way of dividends, interest, lower prices or increased investments, it should be able to continue its momentum. And, by turning-the-corner a second time, the organization will build value in the third dimension, with its Employees.

Turning-the-corner into the third dimension may be difficult to visualize. Consider the box in Figure 6. Assume first that an organization made its way along the X-axis, or in a direction that was growing the value of X fastest (i.e. focused on improving Shareholders perceptions first). Turning-the-corner allowed the organization to address the needs of Customers and begin following a path roughly parallel to the Y-axis but out in zone III where Shareholders' needs are also being met. Turning-the-corner the second time would put the organization on a path that is coming out of the page in a direction that increases the size of the cube (and its Z value).

Fig. 6 Physical–Social Pathway to Wealth (X–Y–Z)

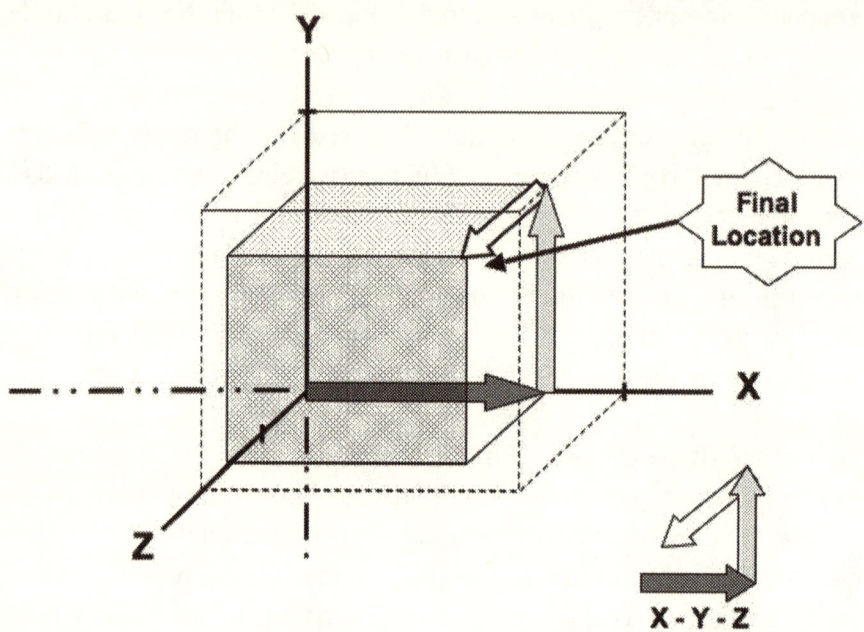

Physical—Causal organizations differ from their first cousins (Physical-Social) in that they rank Employees second, ahead of Customers. This notion of putting Customers last is counter intuitive in many markets today. However, a select group of manufacturers and other Physical Organizations that create significant differentiation in their products through innovation follow this second pathway.

Cutting-edge high tech, bio-tech and niche pharmaceutical companies compete utilizing their core production capabilities and by introducing new, innovative products that make a difference. Large capital investments are needed in plant and equipment making Shareholders of primary concern to the management of these organizations. However, without their motivated, expert Employees, these enterprises would fail.

All Physical entities follow similar paths in stage one. They will drive towards increasing the value of X. However, Physical-Causal organizations will turn-the-corner and look to take care of Employees second. This path will take the organization from traveling along the X-axis to rocketing roughly parallel to the Z-axis. This transition is a very delicate and difficult one to engineer. Managers must work with Shareholders to set appropriate expectations while the organization turns-the-corner. With more resources invested in Employees, the organization's Cause should be forwarded. Expert staffs will create innovations that increase the value of the organization.

With contented Shareholders and a strong pipeline of innovative products in development, the organization will be able to turn-the-corner once again. Management, working closely with Shareholders and Employees, begin to redirect resources into Customer relationships, brands, and other Social Assets. If the investments pay off, Customers will be motivated to purchase products (at cost-plus or premium prices) and tell others about them. (***Note:*** All of these hypothetical organizations illustrated build value in the third dimension to the same point in the Inspirational Zone IV, but none operate in the state of Euphoria IV+, denoted by the flash at the corner of the dotted box/cube.)

Fig. 7 Physical–Causal Pathway to Wealth (X–Z–Y)

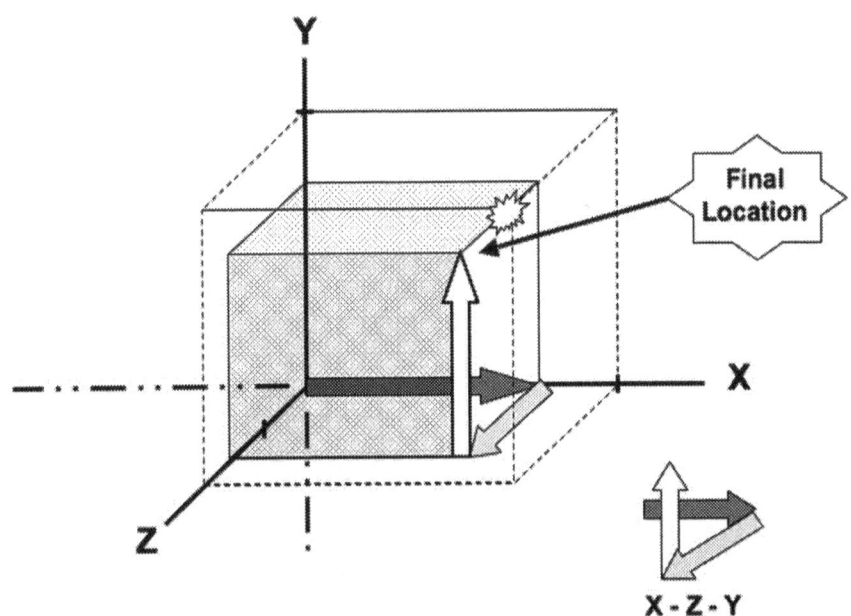

* * *

Author's Note: Building value by progressing from Zone I to Zones II, III or IV is not an easy organizational feat. However, ***maintaining an organization*** in one of the advanced zones is even more difficult. Manufacturing organizations that have turned both corners build substantial value in the eyes of all primary stakeholders. To maintain and increase that value, however, they must continue to manage and meet (or exceed) the expectations of those primary stakeholders. By monitoring where the organization lies on this chart, a management team will be able to direct scarce resources appropriately. They might have to rebuild failing plants, relationships, or morale if the company slips backward on its path.

Manufacturing entities like Johnson & Johnson and DuPont that invest heavily in their physical plants, their brands and technologies, and their people are impressive organizations to watch. These organizations operate in the third dimension where assets have to be leveraged in a complex balance in order to maintain their impressive positions.

* * *

Social ¡POW!s

Social Organizations should make being the best-in-class for their service offerings in their targeted market a primary goal. Their service offerings could be convenience, quality, brand or value. Social Organizations, like their Physical counterparts, will start at the zero point on the chart, where all stakeholders are neutral. Social Organizations will first invest to impress their primary stakeholders. Scarce resources will be heavily allocated towards the needs of Customers. These organizations should push to improve their positive position on the Y-axis in their attempts to gain market and mindshare. Once the enterprise meets the expectations of its Customers, turning-the-corner becomes the next priority.

Turning-the-corner for Social Organizations requires handling stakeholders carefully. Customer expectations must be managed so that high grades continue through the transition. The new direction will depend on the type of organization, either Social-Causal or Social-Physical. After turning-the-corner, these organizations will either track parallel to the Z-axis or the X-axis accordingly.

Social—Causal organizations put their Customers first and recognize that their Employees contribute significantly to those relationships. These organizations should follow a path similar to the one illustrated in Figure 8. They will travel along the Y-axis first and then turn towards improving their position relative to the Z-axis.

Social-Causal enterprises like law practices, advertising agencies and consulting firms strive to be known as the best at providing their particular type of service to their targeted audience. These organizations treat Customers like royalty, and by meeting or exceeding their expectations receive loyalty and accolades. Sales efforts for these service-oriented enterprises can be very expensive, so retaining a stable Customer base is an important economic advantage. Turn-over is expensive! Happy Customers also market the agency very effectively. With customer expectations met, management can afford to allocate a larger amount of resources to Employees.

Employees in these Social-Causal organizations are extremely important. Stars will develop strong relationships with their clients. To retain stars and minimize the risk of losing them and their Customers, managers attempt to meet their expectations on a regular basis. Employees in these service-based organizations will want to believe in what they are offering. They will be driven by an intoxicating mission. And will expect a fair compensation.

Once Customers and Employees needs are met, Shareholders will be afforded a bite of the apple. Fortunately, these organizations require little capital and so leaving Shareholders until last is manageable. This last stage of the developmental path requires the second corner to be turned, pointing the enterprise parallel to the X-axis.

Fig. 8   Social–Causal Pathway to Wealth (Y–Z–X)

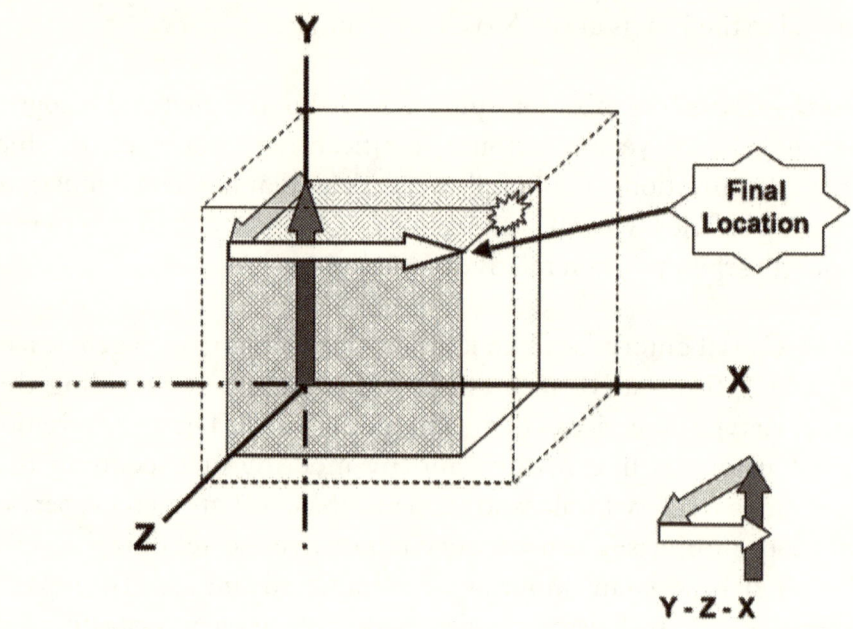

Social—Physical organizations rank their Customers first, but place their Physical Assets and their Shareholders above Employees. Social-Physical enterprises thrive when supported by strong Customer relationships. But they also need deep pocketed financial sponsors to fund the initial building of Physical Assets. Examples of Social-Physical operations include product-based retailers like department stores and Physical Asset-based service organizations like hotels and fitness clubs.

Healthy merchandisers recognize the importance of their Customers. Retailers like Nordstrom, Wal*Mart and the Gap all put Customers first despite their different value propositions and strategies. Successful retailers understand that the needs of their Customers must be met. Products must be available, positioned poignantly, and valued correctly. Outlets will be built to service targeted markets. Location, size, layout and fixturing will be important to the Customer's ultimate shopping experience. Employees are important in higher-end retailer models, but even in those operations, Employees will rank third in importance.

Social-Physical organizations should first move along the Y-axis in an effort to meet the expectations of their primary stakeholder. As these enterprises seek to impress their Customers, they may need to temporarily disappoint Employees and Shareholders. Scarce resources will need to be concentrated on the primary stakeholder. Smart managers will fight to make this Temporarily Tolerable position as brief as possible and push hard to turn-the-first-corner. After the organization turns-the-corner and shoots along parallel to the X-axis, it will be leveraging significant portions of its assets to the benefit of its Shareholders.

Fig. 9   Social–Physical Pathway to Wealth (Y–X–Z)

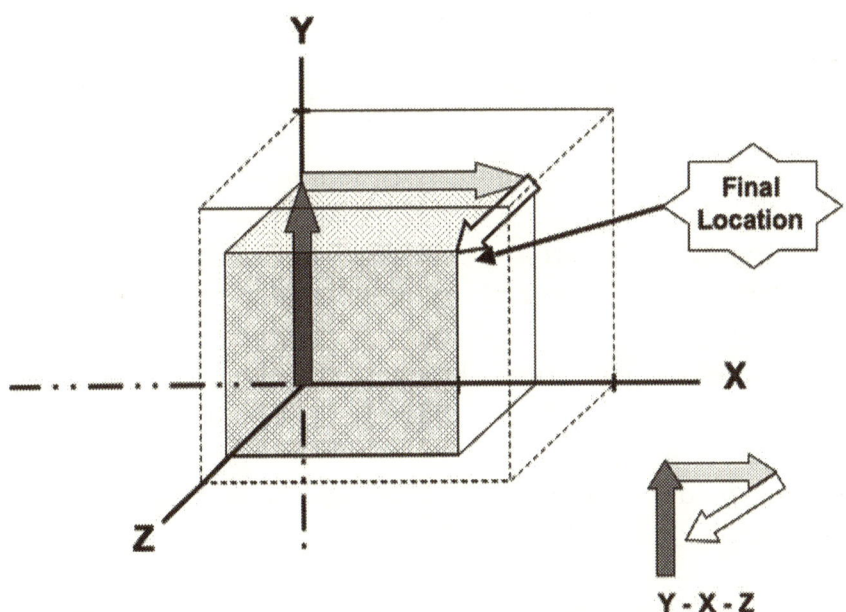

Once Shareholders' expectations are met, the organization should redirect a portion of its wealth creating efforts to its Employees. This second turning-of-the-corner will have the enterprise heading parallel to the Z-axis, in a very positive direction. The closer the organization gets to meeting the needs of its Employees, the larger the cube and value will be created. Inspired Employees will establish cost reduction and quality improvement mechanisms, fuel innovation and increase productivity.

Causal ¡POW!s

Causal Organizations recognize their Employees first. Cause-based organizations are fueled by missions and cultural programs that support powerful communal objectives and values. Employees in these organizations should be driven to make the world a better place by serving others.

Causal enterprises may hold their Shareholders (e.g. sponsors, donors) and Customers (e.g. patients, parishioners, students) in high esteem, but Employees (including volunteers) will create the most value for these organizations. To impress and energize Employees, administrations should first leverage core assets to support and maximize the effectiveness of those Employees. They want to "do good". By helping them do more good, many of their expectations will be met.

As a Causal Organization improves its standing with its Employees, it will move along the Z-axis in a positive direction. When appropriate, the enterprise should turn-the-corner and move along parallel to the X or Y-axis depending on its ranking of its remaining two stakeholders.

Causal—Social organizations like many service-based non-profits will follow a path similar to the one illustrated in Figure 10. These cause-driven organizations will have little need for Physical Assets and rank their stakeholders accordingly: Employees first, then Customers, then Shareholders.

Causal-Social organizations as illustrated should first move along the Z-axis as they work to meet the needs of their Employees. Investments in work environments, productivity training/tools and support mechanisms will energize Employees. Once Employees catch the bug, resource should be allocated towards Customers (Y-axis).

Mentoring, tutoring and counseling organizations are all examples of entities that must first recruit, then train and finally energize their workforces (most of which could be volunteer or low paid positions). These enterprises must then build its trust and profile in their targeted markets. These organizations are funded to have an impact on the world. The more people seeking help from the enterprise, the more potential good might be achieved.

Donors and other Shareholders are important. Their voices should be heard. However, a Causal-Social organization that has motivated employees and that is a trusted resource in its community should not have to beg for funds. Shareholders (donors) should invest (give) based on the demonstrated capabilities of the enterprise and its motivated management and work force. The more capital raised, the more resources available, the greater the potential good to be created by the staff. The more good created (in an efficient manner) the more pleased Shareholders become (X-axis), the more donations will flow, and the larger the wealth (and cube) that will be created.

Fig. 10 Causal–Social Pathway to Wealth (Z–Y–X)

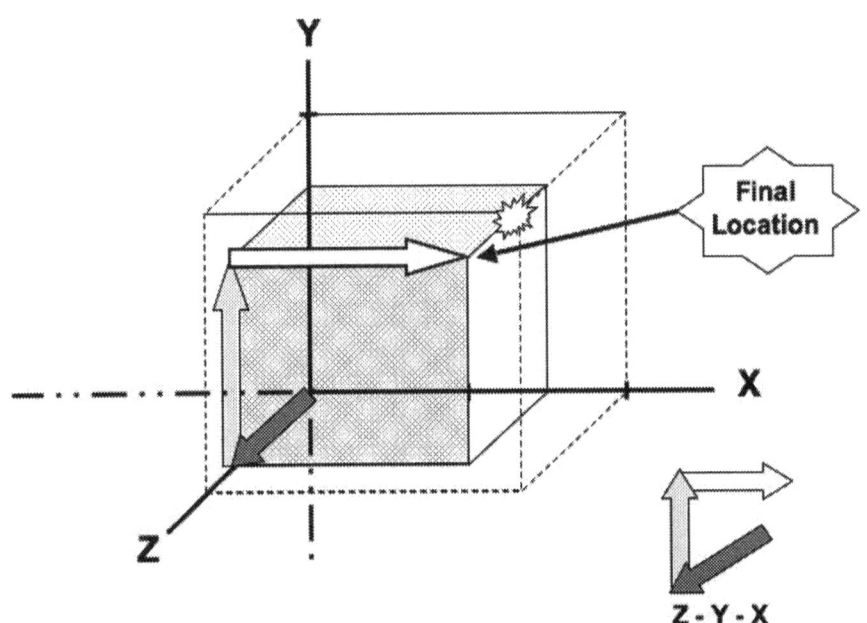

The *Causal—Physical* category includes many of our tax-funded, public benefit organizations. These entities are also cause-based and service-oriented, but have significant amounts of Physical Assets required for their wealth creation. Hospitals, universities and other asset-based institutions like the military, law enforcement and emergency response operations (e.g. fire) could be classified as Causal-Physical enterprises.

Causal-Physical organizations should first listen to the desires of their Employees. These doctors, nurses, professors, teachers, officers and firefighters all desire to improve the world and are inspired by the prospects of achieving as much as possible. In order to deliver the service that is needed by their communities, large pools of Physical Assets must be leveraged. The need to fund these assets places Shareholders such as donors and taxpayers second on the list of stakeholders. Organizations that efficiently leverage their Physical Assets and provide convincing returns on the capital deployed will please Shareholders, travel parallel to the X-axis and build value.

Fig. 11 Causal–Physical Pathway to Wealth (Z–X–Y)

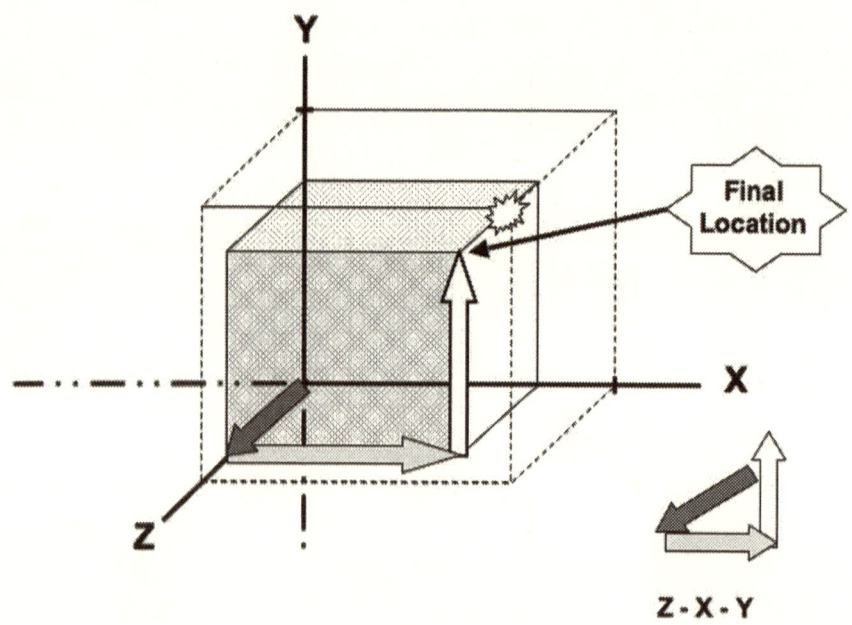

The majority of Customers helped by these organizations will be in need and have little choice where to get serviced. Many will not even pay for their own care directly. For both these reasons and due to the importance of Physical Assets, Shareholders (often taxpayers) will outrank Customers in importance. However, to maximize wealth creation, Customers expectations must be met. This will push the box on the chart out along the Y-axis and represent significant value creation for the organization and its community.

CHAPTER 6

¡*POW!*S THAT WOW!—
REAL WORLD EXAMPLES

Organizations that execute successful ¡*POW!*s are exciting to experience. The growth in value as these enterprises transition from one direction on their paths to another is fantastic. The momentum created by these organizations as they build wealth in the third dimension is incredible.

I have lead, experienced and/or witnessed the thrill of many turn-arounds, start-ups and developing entities. I'd like to share a few vignettes from a number of those experiences to help bring this management framework to life. I've selected these examples from a broad range of organizational types to illustrate the applicability of this model to all organizations.

Physical—Causal: On the Rack Track (X-Z-Y)

One of my most rewarding organizational experiences occurred while leading a mid-sized manufacturing company that specialized in luggage racks for cars and trucks. This organization had a colorful history filled with entrepreneurial flare and zaniness befitting a company that was founded in coastal Northern California.

My journey with the company began with an executive recruiter introducing me to the owners. The company had been bought by an investment group from the original entrepreneurs four years prior, after a meteoric rise in sales. Unfortunately, the four years post acquisition were not as rewarding. They were marked with tepid sales growth, financial losses and tough fiscal measures. Shareholder frustration grew to a boiling point and a management change was demanded. The recruiter was hired and I was contacted.

I can still remember stepping through the front doors of that organization for the first time. The colorful past was painted on the walls (in the form of massive murals) but the heart and soul of the company had been ripped out. It struck me in an instant that the key to creating significant value with this company was through reawakening its collective spirit.

This was a classic manufacturing company. We made metal and plastic products. You could have any color you wanted, provided it was black or some shade of grey. Obviously, I had stepped into a Physical Organization. Shareholders ruled with an iron fist. When I arrived, their grasp was so tight that they frequented debates over everything (even discussions about the piece price of rivets at less than a penny a pop!)

It was evident that we had a lot of work to do. Shareholders were Upset and they had lost confidence in management. Our Customers (specialty retailers), an independent vocal bunch, were expressing concerns over product availability, the lack of innovation and poor quality. Our Employees were distraught and distracted. They were concerned for their jobs, which was a big deal in this small town. And yet, we did have a core following of consumers, loyal enthusiasts for whom we made arguably the best car racks on the market.

I did not have a specific ¡*POW!* approach in mind when I took over as CEO. I had not yet experienced enough organizations to understand the six patterns in organizational decision making. In fact, I was in an initial quandary over the correct ranking of stakeholders. My training suggested a ranking that put Shareholders first, followed by Customers, with Employees last. This would have been typical for most branded consumer product companies (a Physical-Social classification) and be consistent with what was currently being practiced at the company. But my heart told me to move Employees up in the ranking. I followed my heart.

I now recognize that the classification of this entity as a Physical-Causal organization should have been more obvious. The company was fueled by product innovation. Our designers created products that they wanted. They were product enthusiasts and experts. Our pricing was not based on the market, but based on our cost to make the product. Whatever our cost was, we added a reasonable margin and rounded that calculation to establish our price (i.e. a cost-plus approach). Clearly, the company was a technology-driven, manufacturing company. We generated large value from our Physical Assets, but we also needed a cause to inspire our Employees' competitive drive and creativity.

So what path did we take? We began in the Unacceptable area. All of our core stakeholders were either Disappointed or Upset. Very quickly management constructed a business plan that reset expectations of Shareholders. This was not going to be a quick fix. Nor would it reach their initial goals. We also asked that all positive cash flow generated to be reinvested in the company until the turn-around was complete. The Shareholders accepted.

The plan was achievable, but far from easy. The first page of the business plan summarized our financial goals for the next five years. The next three pages, however, spoke to our collective mission, values and quality philosophies. The remaining pages built bridges between the first page and the following three. The plan illustrated in slide form how we, the

Employees, could deliver on our promise to the Shareholders by doing what we wanted to do—by creating great product and making a positive impact on the world.

The creation of the business plan was an important process in rebuilding Employee morale. Management and a small group of Employees (who were important leaders in a cultural sense) went offsite into a cabin in the redwoods. We tossed boomerangs during breaks from our heated debates about the purpose of our organization. Profit was not considered a good thing by many at this company!

The second, third and fourth pages of the business plan were powerful, guiding tenants for our organization. Our quality statement, for example, was a promise to ourselves and a bold statement to our owners: "We will exceed the expectations of our customers, friends and families". Skeptical Employees heard the cry, tested our resolve and then climbed aboard.

Little-by-little Employees rediscovered their passion. Faster and faster our improvements came. Within six-months we had converted a money-losing operation into a money maker. In less than 12-months we launched industry changing products, something that we hadn't done in years. By the second year our growth was double what our Shareholders had hoped for and our profitability was growing 40-percent a year.

Management successfully led the company along the X-axis and turned-the-corner with pizzazz. Shareholders remained contented as we diverted more resources into Employees (Z-axis). Soon we were exceeding the expectations of our Employees. However, we did not bump salaries significantly or pay out huge bonuses. Instead we invested more into R&D capabilities (better computers and simulators), improved manufacturing equipment and gave more donations to our community. We were a Physical-Causal Organization. We had to invest in our Physical Assets to reduce costs and improve quality. Our Employees wanted to be fairly compensated, but they were more energized by investments that supported our missions of being the best and making a positive impact than by large payouts.

As the years went by, the company delivered more innovative products more often. Customers lauded our designs, quality and delivery (Y-axis). We filed for and were granted many patents. We won awards from most of our top customers for our service. Despite being stingy with our marketing dollars and increasing our prices every six months, we blasted into and then flourished in the third dimension. Eventually we were exceeding the expectations of all three core stakeholders: Shareholders, Employees and Customers.

Our organization operated in the state of Euphoria for a wonderful period. This was exhilarating for Employees and a very valuable position for the Shareholders who realized a record setting valuation for the company in an auction. Unfortunately, shortly after the sale, our bubble was burst. Our new Shareholders had very different expectations and positioned the importance of brands and Customers above Employees. And the box imploded once again.

Physical—Social: Cutting through the Clutter (X-Y-Z)

After selling one of my start-ups to a much larger company, I was again free to consult. One progressive CEO, after reading my book *"Business Euphoria—Powering Relational Organizations with Gangs, Gall and Gossip"* asked me to come in to work with him and his management team on transitioning their company. This was a healthy, mid-sized knife manufacturer that was growing at a steady clip.

There was a different feel to the culture in this organization from my rack experience. Both companies were extremely successful, located in the Pacific Northwest and of similar size. They both sold through sporting good departments and had strong consumer brands. And yet the Employee-inspired magic appeared to be lacking within the walls of this organization.

The knife manufacturer was being run like a classic consumer products company. (In fact, key senior management members came from the beer industry.) And it was obvious that their model worked. They put Shareholders first, Customers second and Employees third. They developed reasonable expectations with their Shareholders and met (or exceeded) them consistently. Significant resources were invested into Physical Assets to make them more efficient and improve quality. But most of their success came from turning-the-corner and investing in Customers. This management team understood the value of strong brands and the power of Customer relationships. Once Shareholders were satiated, executives redirected resources into their storied brand and service capabilities. And sales shot through the roof.

Their product line was very macho—knives and hunting equipment. But it was also very fashion-oriented. Knives happen to be the equivalent of jewelry for many men (like watches and sun glasses). And we all know the Social importance of brands and design in fashion-oriented products and industries. To increase the Social value of their products and organization, management invested in large media campaigns. They also purchased and licensed many designs from hot product designers in the field. And they invested in their Customer relationships. Customers responded by ranking them their number one supplier repeatedly.

To free up more of the incremental cash flow that was being generated and allow those resources to be directed into building Social Assets, the company began sourcing its additional volume requirements off shore. Over time, the organization became more Social and slightly less Physical. They began investing relatively more into Social Assets like their brand than Physical ones like buildings and equipment.

The management team understood the importance of an inspired workforce. They inherited a plant with Disappointed Employees and an active union. After product and marketing successes, they invested in their Employees. The company began offering better benefits, improved management practices and consistent communications. And morale improved significantly. There were plenty of bumps in the road, there was significant turn-over, but eventually this organization began to grow in the third dimension as well.

Management traveled the classic Physical-Social path and won! They created significant wealth for their Shareholders, Customers and ultimately for Employees. These managers had a formula (X-Y-Z) that was very successful and were recruited to repeat their success in another organization owned by the same Shareholders.

*   *   *

Author's Note: Debating the classification of an organization can be a very powerful activity for management. This discussion forces management teams to define organizational wealth, prioritize stakeholders, clarify their needs and measure their opinions. Although I have not yet found an objective set of measures that would allow for simple, absolute classifications, I am excited by the value created by the current, collaborative, classification process.

The classification debate required by this framework, in its current form, can be very rewarding. Some organizations should be very easy to classify, others will require more thought. Those additional discussions can spawn important strategic insights. I remember many clarifying revelations from similar processes. One created an important distinction between two manufacturing companies with which I was involved.

I was a board member of an innovative, lifejacket manufacturing company. This enterprise had been created by its founder in response to a terrible loss he had experienced—His best friend drowned in a boating accident. The Physical nature of this manufacturing organization was obvious. So too was its cause—It was created to save lives! The Employees were passionate about their communal purpose. Innovative products were designed, manufactured and marketed in order to help others. Obviously, this was a Physical-Causal organization.

One of the companies I helped found made cause-based jewelry. Remember those yellow, rubber "LiveSTRONG" bracelets? Well, we didn't make those, but something similar. This enterprise designed and manufactured customizable, metal jewelry (e.g. anodized and custom etched aluminum rings) that allowed clubs, schools, universities and other Causal Organizations to express their beliefs and raise money for their causes. We were a manufacturing entity that had motivated Employees. But we put our Customer's causes before our own. Although our product was "cause-based" we weren't. We were a Physical-Social organization.

*   *   *

Social—Causal: Teaching as a Service (Y-Z-X)

By the time I joined the management team of a for-profit education company, the organization had already been rocked by a catastrophic shift in the market brought on by 9/11. This was a novel assignment for me. I had just come from a consulting engagement with a university, but I had not yet lead a teaching institution.

My first actions as CEO included taking the temperature of Employees, Customers and Shareholders (while getting up a steep learning curve on the regulatory requirements we had to operate within). After listening to numerous stakeholders and several consultants in the industry, it became obvious to me: For-profit education enterprises are very different from their collegial counter-parts. We were a for-profit, service-based business. Not a university or school.

Customers (students) paid us a lot of money to help them obtain specific job-enriching credentials. This was all about teaching them important skills, not about shaping their minds. Our students on average were 35 to 40 years old, working and supporting a family. They invested in our brand, our reputation for turning out top talent, and in our strong record of placing our students in good jobs.

This organization drew most of its funding from Customers. Students paid their tuition at the beginning of their programs with credit cards or with financing from lending institutions. We operated the company on that cash. We had large operating expenses for leases, salaries and advertising, but very few Physical Assets. We leased our eight campuses, our administrative offices, computers, software, desks and chairs. So, despite being a for-profit venture, our Shareholders ranked last. We chose to place Customers first, Employees second and Shareholders third.

Shareholders (and the banks) were Upset. We were operating on a shoe string with many liabilities piled on our Balance Sheet. Employees were exhausted and underpaid. During the heroic efforts to save the enterprise, many Employees were let go. Those remaining saw titles, responsibilities and workloads increased, but times were lean. Despite the battles that raged during the downsizing, however, management never lost sight of their primary responsibility: To take care of the Customer.

Despite our tight times, we always found money to advertise, to build our brand and attract students. We also invested in our very best instructors. We worked them hard, but paid enough to retain top talent. These teachers delivered the value that our Customers paid for. Management and many administrative employees had salaries frozen or reduced. Vendors and landlords were paid when and if money came available. Banks and Shareholders watched, anxious that the enterprise remain viable.

Fortunately, management chose its ranking well. We worked from a significantly negative position relative to Shareholders (X-axis) and Employees (Y-axis) and began to rebuild organizational value. We created a list of all the people and organizations that had invoiced us for work done. We ranked them according to their importance to our current operations. We created a financial recovery plan and then shared it with our Shareholders, banks, landlords and vendors. We reset expectations regarding who we could pay and how much we would pay on a regular basis. And then we went to work on rebuilding our organization.

For two years the organization operated hand-to-mouth. During that time it managed to get back into compliance with government authorities, paid off most of its vendors and attracted a new group of investors. Miraculously, the organization had survived certain death and managed to build significant wealth in difficult market conditions. It traveled along the Y-axis (regularly meeting the needs of Customers), up parallel to the Z-axis (by giving hope to Employees) and eventually developed exciting plans for the X-axis. The company had developed enough value to attract financial suitors and an exit strategy for Shareholders and the banks.

Social—Physical: Retailing Routes (Y-X-Z)

Several of my assignments have taken me into struggling retail operations. I have managed a small retailer and consulted to a number of larger ones. Despite their size differences, rankings remained consistent for stakeholders of product-based retailers: Customers first, Shareholders second, Employees third.

Employees play a part in all service-based organizations, but they are least important in Social-Physical organizations like retailers of merchandise. Retailers provide a service to their Customers—Merchants offer products that interest Customers in locations that are convenient, fun, clean and easy to navigate. They allow Customers to touch, try and compare their products. And they offer some assistance in making purchasing decisions.

Retailers strive to become known as the best (easiest, cheapest, coolest) place to shop for their targeted Customers. They must attract potential Customers and then convert them into purchasers. Retailers invest heavily in Social Assets like brands, locations and advertisements in an effort to build their relevance to their target market. And they stock significant quantities of the desired product in stores (Physical Assets) in order to meet the immediate demands of browsing Customers.

Retail turn-arounds start with reconnecting with Customers. I have been amazed time-and-again by the inability of retail managers to describe who their Customers were or define what they expected in actionable details. Who shops your store and why? Retailers wilt without a clear vision of who they are trying to attract, or an understanding of what their Customers are searching for. My assignments have begun the same each time: By talking with a lot of Customers.

All of the retail managers I have worked with have been smart, personable and aggressive. They have to be. They have very difficult jobs. They attempt to optimize service-oriented, Social enterprises that are constrained by Physical Assets. Customers are fickle and ever-changing. Physical Assets are typically static. Unfortunately, many retailers fail to adapt with their evolving Customers' needs as styles, shopping patterns and demographics shift. Continually meeting the needs of Customers requires these organizations to be aware and adaptable. Product offerings, brands and communications must remain fresh and connected. And locations must be adjusted as Customers and communities change.

Shareholders fund Balance Sheets that support large inventory requirements and operating leases, both important cornerstones of the service being offered. Employees are important but more as a differentiating tactic—Icing on the cake. Is the retailer a high-end, service-oriented operation where ample floor staffing is expected? Or is the retailer a discount operation that offers low prices and bright signage for self-help? The service and the retailer will first be rated on its location and product offerings (Will we stop to shop?) before we worry about Employee interaction. If Employees are adequate, Customer expectations can typically be met by having the right product, easily accessible, at a reasonable price.

To optimize the value potential of a retailer, it is important to start with Customers (Y-axis) and then work Shareholders (X-axis) in an effort to encourage additional support for the capital requirements of Social-Physical organizations. I am an Employee advocate, and Employees will make the final difference in the experience of the Customer (and help build significant value). But the retail competition is setting a very low bar.

Causal—Physical: Teaching as a Mission (Z-X-Y)

I was shocked when I heard comments like: "We don't have Customers..." and "We won't change what we are doing. We came hear to teach!" I was facilitating a dialog amongst university professors that were facing tough demands from a new administration. Frustrations were running high and compromise did not seem possible.

I had been invited into the university to help professors discover a new direction that would resonate with the administration, students, alumni, and the community. The university was going through a difficult financial period exacerbated by declining enrollments and a State budget crisis. The new administration was fighting to implement a shift in direction for the university that it felt would improve their current situation.

During the semester preceding my assignment, several icy exchanges had occurred between the new President and his tenured faculty. The President expected more research, scholarship and community interaction out of the professors. The faculty countered that this was a teaching university first and added that budget cuts had increased teaching loads to the point where additional activities proved impossible.

I spent many hours one summer with faculty members debating who their stakeholders were and what those stakeholders expected. What the faculty's collective purpose was. What responsibilities they had and to whom. We discussed what constituted value and how to maximize the value they and the university created.

Those were eye-opening discussions for me. The room was filled with intelligence, pride and energy. These were committed, passionate

Employees that wanted to make a difference. But they did not agree with the administration's demands and would not budge. And they didn't have to! They were tenured faculty, in a public university and most belonged to a union.

During that summer I came to realize the importance of Employees in Causal Organizations. For cause-based organizations to create wealth, the Employees must be motivated. They are the most important stakeholder group. Their needs and desires must be aligned with the mission of the organization for value to be maximized. We spent the summer discussing, creating and finally combining the interests of faculty with the direction of the administration.

In Causal-Physical organizations Shareholders rank second and Customers last. That Customers (i.e. the students) rank last sounds counter intuitive. Weren't the professors driven to help the students? Wasn't the university funded to teach the students? Yes and yes, but when push comes to shove, students rank last. Tenured professors will do as they wish. Administrators will cut budgets, services and classes as needed. And students will piece together the best class offerings available for their degrees.

To create maximum value the university will need to meet the expectations of professors and staff (Z-axis). With their energy and commitment supporting administrative efforts, budgets will be met and funding drives successful (X-axis). An inspired faculty will energize the students (Y-axis), attract new recruits and together the stakeholders will create significant wealth.

Causal—Social: Serving Others (Z-Y-X)

Cause-based service organizations help many people in need. Many of us have volunteered in not-for-profits that can be classified as Causal-Social. I have volunteered time to tutor, mentor, coach, build homes, clean parks, and renovate trails. I donate my time and energy to organizations that I believe in. These organizations often have very low capital needs and can rank their Customers second, right after their Employees (staff and volunteers).

I sat on the board of a specialized after-school program that was supported by large corporate sponsors and senior community leaders from the populous, troubled neighborhoods it served. This was an organization that had big hitters supporting it, but it was the Employees that called the shots.

Early in the development of the organization the board elected to recruit the best, most committed talent available to lead the enterprise. The director that was hired motivated his staff, recruited volunteers, inspired donors and thrilled the children. Following the direction of a determined and talented leader, the organization thrived. Employees were devoted (Z-axis), communities were thrilled (Y-axis) and donors were excited (X-axis). The organization was built on the passion of its staff. And it was run professionally with strict operating procedures, training requirements and tight budgets.

Significant value was created by the organization. So much that neighboring cities wanted it to expand into their communities. And donors wanted to fund that growth. But the board halted the expansion plans. The leader had voiced concerns about his staff's ability to manage the rapid growth. They had not yet trained a solid enough team to leverage their managerial talent across large distances and many cities. So the organization operated at a perfect size, exceeding the expectations of everyone involved until the Employees were ready to grow again.

¡POW!s that OW!

Not all organizations choose the correct path. Organizations on the wrong pathway are easy to spot. They will typically be underperforming or failing. I am often hired to lead or encourage organizations back onto and then along the correct track. Unfortunately, not all of my assignments meet my expectations for value creation.

For one particularly painful assignment, I was recruited to run a mid-sized Physical-Social organization (X-Y-Z). It was a classic consumer products company that had lost its way. Hemorrhaging cash, I was parachuted in as CEO to restructure the Balance Sheet and lead an operational turn-around. I was hopeful in the beginning. Shareholders supported us. We appeared to have solid products, a strong brand, well developed channels, and a professional sales force. I soon learned, however, that the company was in worse shape than I was led to believe. Not only were our books cooked to inflate results, our products were tired, and our brand was in decline.

Management created a business plan and reset our financial sponsors' expectations. The Shareholders contributed additional capital, but only the bare minimum. We began investing our limited resources to win back the trust and confidence of our Customers. However, we had to overcome years of Customer abuse resulting from management decisions that had put Employees first, Shareholders second and Customers third (Oops! This should have read: Shareholders, Customers then Employees). And we needed to reorganize. We were pregnant with overpaid, pampered Employees.

Despite significant effort, our turn-around ran out of time. Our most important stakeholder, the Shareholders (an equity fund), needed to move on. Too many bombs were dropped in and around our company during our voyage, slowing our recovery efforts. We had to settle with developing less value than desired in a constrained time period. Shareholders opted for a clean exit after we had corrected our path, but left some of the upside opportunity to the next group of Shareholders.

. . . *The Wrong Flight Path*

Airlines are Social-Physical organizations (Y-Z-X). They perform a service—They carry us from one place to another. And they utilize massive flotillas of Physical Assets (e.g. aircraft, cargo trucks, equipment and computers) to perform this service. Based on this classification, I would expect them to place Customers first, Shareholders second and Employees third.

It doesn't surprise me that most Employees of the large carriers belong to unions. Given their tertiary ranking, a collective voice might help during negotiations. However, I am baffled by the poor treatment of Customers by the large airlines. I am a regular Customer. I travel a lot as part of my job. And I am often Disappointed with my travel experiences (despite my low expectations).

These large carriers appear to be run like giant "passenger-mile" factories driven to optimize throughput to appease Shareholders (X-Y-Z). Customers are squeezed into smaller packages (i.e. seats) to maximize the production potential of each batch (i.e. flight). Basics like soda and food are rationed or stripped completely. And prices are increased at every possible opportunity (except on fares to Timbuktu on Sundays). Wake-up guys, you are flying on the wrong flight path! You are not producing widgets, you are providing a service!

Meanwhile many regional carriers operate dynamic Social-Physical operations that are creating significant wealth for their stakeholders. These nimble, Customer-oriented, service organizations provide clean, dependable transportation, at a fair price and with flair! Motivated Employees buy into the purpose of their organizations, remain relatively union-free, and enhance the flying experience. And Customers reward the Southwest's and Jet Blue's of the world with loyalty and praise.

. . . Causal Calamities

Causal organizations should rank Employees first. And administrations should be working hard to meet or exceed the expectations of these important stakeholders. Yet, many of the Causal-Physical organizations (Z-X-Y) I have experienced as a consultant, Customer, Shareholder or Employee (e.g. schools, universities, hospitals) attract unions. Which begs the question—Why would Employees need unions if they had the top ranking and their needs were being met?

According to this expectations-based model, many of our Causal-Physical organizations must be underperforming. No organization could be maximizing wealth creation if its primary stakeholder is Disappointed or Upset. In fact, many of our important institutions may actually be destroying value—Returning far less than what stakeholders expect for their investments.

The good news is that many of us recognize the potential of our public benefit organizations. And we are willing to help in their transformations. The bad news is that many of our well-meaning neighbors (who might not have read this book) will push the wrong buttons and call for change too aggressively. They may demand tough cultural shifts, force fiscal discipline measures, require changes to staff, and Upset Employees unproductively in the process. Perhaps the red cover of this book will prompt some seasonal gifting this winter that will help prevent future Causal calamities.

CHAPTER 7

ADJUSTING ¡POW!S—
SHAPING YOUR DESTINY

Organizations of the same type will follow similar pathways to organizational wealth. But some of these enterprises will navigate the path more easily than others. Each management team has a set group of assets and stakeholders at any given point in time. However, skilled managers will influence expectations, shift the balance of assets and even adjust stakeholder make-up over time.

Organizations within the same classification will need to address the needs of all three stakeholder groups. They will all have to leverage scarce asset pools towards these ends. And the most efficient path to creating maximum value will be the same. However, if managers can lower the expectations of one class of stakeholders, even temporarily, resources will be freed up to address another class. With effective communications and energetic recruitment, management could affect the make-up of its stakeholder groups over time. And with subtle or bold moves, executives can build a different mix of assets through redirecting resource investments.

These changes may increase the likelihood that the organization will build wealth. But if the stakeholders of these organizations retain their original ranking, these tweaks will not adjust the actual *¡POW!* of the organization. Because this is an expectations-based model, if the relative rankings of stakeholders remain the same, the organization's pathway will not change. The organization will still need to meet the expectations of each of its stakeholders in turn. Some of those expectations may now be easier to meet or exceed, assets might be better aligned with their needs, but the most efficient pathway to increasing wealth will be to address the stakeholders in order.

Influencing expectations, adjusting asset balances and recruiting stakeholders is the job of management. Strong managers do not just operate with the tools they were given. They will push, prod and pull in order to improve their organizations' probability for success. This is what they are paid to do.

Examples of asset-bases being tweaked are evident in the tactical investments of enterprises. To improve our chances for success at the rack company we first became "more Physical". We increased our investment in Physical Assets. We became more vertically integrated by purchasing more machinery. This allowed us to reduce costs and improve quality. It also increased the expectations of the Shareholders. But we remained a Physical-Causal company (X-Z-Y).

The knife company chose to become "more Social". It did the opposite to the rack company. As the enterprise grew, rather than investing in more Physical Assets to build manufacturing capacity, it sourced the additional products in Asia. Without the need to invest in additional machinery, management had more resources to invest in its brand initiatives and in its Customer relationships. Although the knife company increased the profile of its Customers, it remained a Physical-Social organization (i.e. Shareholders kept their top ranking, X-Y-Z).

Many product retailers are attempting to be more nimble. Investment in virtual stores has become common place. A web-based outlet is a very Social addition to the asset base of these Social-Physical retailers (Y-X-Z). These additional operations build Social Assets like brands and Customer relationships. They are very adaptable. And they demand little in the way of Physical Assets or capital—Often, a Physical location is not needed nor is additional product inventory. This shift should address the needs of Customers without increasing expectations of Shareholders significantly (or change its organizational classification).

In the for-profit education company, we worked hard to increase our flexibility and reduce our dependence on Physical Assets. We restructured our campus leases, leased rather than purchased equipment and were moving towards additional web-based or home-based instruction. We redirected the capital that would have otherwise been used in the upfront purchase of equipment, computers, systems and software into our brand and service offerings. This adjustment made us more Social and less Physical, but we remained a Social-Causal organization (Y-Z-X).

Many Causal-Physical organizations (Z-X-Y) like hospitals are attempting to reduce their collections of Physical Assets. Improvements in technology are enhancing treatment offerings, but the related equipment is often expensive. Huge capital budgets are required to keep up with equipment improvements. Through leasing and sharing arrangements many of these organizations attempt to offer their Employees the best tools for their trade, while making their asset base more efficient. With careful attention to capital budgets and creative sharing arrangements for Physical Assets, these organizations can become less Physical and meet the needs of Employees and Customers more efficiently.

Many Causal-Social organizations (Z-Y-X) may benefit from becoming more Physical. Constructing a club house, office building (or other infrastructure) or establishing an endowment can have a very positive effect on the value of a cause-based organization. These moves might signal stability for risk-averse, potential volunteers or donors. These organizations might increase their Physical Asset base, but they would remain Causal-Social.

Adjusting the path of an organization requires altering its classification. An organization is classified based on its core assets and its primary stakeholders. So, if an organization is to travel on a new track, major moves would need to take place—Either a change in stakeholder ranking (and assets rebalanced accordingly) or a major shift in assets must occur (and stakeholder rankings adjusted appropriately).

Altering an organization enough to change its ¡*POW!* can be a major and precarious event in the history of an enterprise. The easier adjustments occur within the subgroups. Altering a Physical-Causal (X-Z-Y) to a Physical-Social organization (X-Y-Z) requires switching the rankings of the second and third stakeholders (i.e. Customers move up and Employees move down). This move is typically less extreme and more likely to succeed than when asset balances are shifted significantly or the corresponding top stakeholder loses their dominant position. An example of the latter transformation would require a company going from a primarily Physical entity (e.g. manufacturing company) to a predominantly Social entity (e.g. branded retailer) or to a Causal enterprise (e.g. research & design firm).

These dramatic organizational changes do occur. Anecdotal evidence suggests that these transformations are more likely to succeed, however, if they are part of an organization's strategic development, occurring over a prolonged and planned period rather than abruptly following a significant event like a sale. Unfortunately, I have experienced and seen many organizations thrashed after a sale. New Shareholders that ride in and push the organization onto a different path can have a catastrophic impact.

I described my experience in a Physical-Causal organization that was pushed onto a Physical-Social path (i.e. the rack company). Intellectually, this transition made sense. We were already becoming more market-driven (Social) and less technologically-oriented (Causal) prior to the Shareholder switch. This organization should have been able to build value by leveraging its brand across more products, channels and markets. For many technical consumer product companies, this transformation is a natural progression in their development. But the rapid change that occurred hurt the rack company significantly. Product innovation and quality slumped, critical Employees left, Customers fled and the value of the business plummeted.

The invention of a better "mousetrap" is an obvious starting point for many new manufacturers. An inventor comes up with an idea and makes a few of his contraptions. With feedback from those early prototypes improvements are made. With luck, connections and enthusiasm an entrepreneur might see real demand for the products. Increasing sales volumes should result in resources that can be reinvested back into the organization.

At some point in the development of this mousetrap manufacturing organization, the Board will decide whether to continue proceeding along a Physical-Causal route (one that puts technology and product innovation first), or transition to a Physical-Social one (where a brand is developed and leveraged). Often, as technology companies become larger, they are forced to grow out of their niche, technical markets. At this point, they begin competing for market share with rivals offering similar products. And the importance of Customer relationships (and brands) grows accordingly. This sort of natural, prolonged transformation has a higher likelihood of succeeding than forced, rapid changes.

Another way to *adjust a path* with a greater likelihood of success would be through a large organization "birthing" (or "spinning off") a portion of its operations (that is of critical mass and that differs in organizational type from the "parent"). An example of this sort of transformation includes Physical-Causal organizations (e.g. technology-oriented manufacturing enterprises, X-Z-Y) that split the R&D or consulting arms of their organization from their base business of manufacturing (e.g. IBM). This type of split allows for the original Physical Organization to better focus on its core stakeholders (i.e. Shareholders). And it allows the "new", adolescent Causal or Social organization to develop the appropriate asset base to address the needs of its primary stakeholders (i.e. either Employees or Customers).

These spin-offs can build significant value for the stakeholders. Management in each of the organizations should be able to more efficiently leverage their assets to meet the needs of their core stakeholders. An organization that develops a blend of operational types will struggle to find an effective *¡POW!* Managers will find it difficult to balance the competing interests of stakeholders and friction will build as expectations are missed. Manufacturing companies must put Shareholders first. Consulting firms rank Customers first. And many R&D houses must put their Employees on top. As the original organization develops its non-primary operations, inefficiencies and frustrations will grow. The split allows managers to refocus efforts on their primary stakeholders and more effectively address their needs.

By *merging stakeholders groups*, a group of stakeholders will improve its ranking and the organization might build value more easily. For organizations that have merged stakeholders, management may be able to leverage scarce assets to meet the needs of their stakeholders more efficiently. Instead of three groups of primary stakeholders, managers would only need to communicate with two. The combined stakeholder group would continue to have their separate needs addressed, but these needs will often be aligned. Aligned expectations may allow for more efficient resource allocations. The paths of these organizations will remain the same. However, these organizations might move into the third dimension more quickly.

Merged stakeholders groups are common in entrepreneurial and small organizations that are started and run by a worker/owner. Merged stakeholders also appear to be preferred by some organizational types. Social-Causal organizations (Y-Z-X), for instance, like law, consulting and accounting firms that require a significant brain-trust and little capital are often owned by partners (Shareholders) that are also Employees. These organizations can develop significant wealth by converting their star Employees into partners (Shareholders) and retaining their coveted account base (Customers). Larger professional organizations like investment banks, large accounting and consulting firms do manage to split Shareholders from Employees in events typically geared to cashing-out the original partners. However, these large organizations often struggle with key Employee retention (and related Customer loyalty) after the split.

Co-operatives represent a very interesting example of organizations with merged stakeholders. In one type of these organizations many of the Customers are also the Shareholders. These organizations can be very Physical, very Social, or Cause-dominated. I have experienced successful co-operatives in the retail environment and in the distribution and marketing of agricultural produce. These organizations travel the same paths as their non-merged counterparts, but expectations of merged parties that are consistently aligned can often be met more efficiently (i.e. with less resources expended) than those that might compete more often.

Powerful stakeholders can cause *periods of reversal* in stakeholder rankings. But these organizations are typically in trouble or doomed. Causal Organizations that have administrators forcing compliance on professionals, or donors demanding control of non-profit board rooms are, or will be, in distress. Physical Organizations that are controlled by labor unions, or Social Organizations that are dominated by Shareholders, will likely fall short of their wealth-creating potentials.

Market dynamics will alter the absolute bargaining power of stakeholders and their related expectations. However, within a healthy organization, relative power rankings between stakeholders should remain constant. Shareholders should rank first in Physical organizations, Customers first in Social entities and Employees first in Causal enterprises.

*   *   *

Author's Note: Not all of us want to be served by well meaning, public benefit organizations. Some Customers would rather invest in their special needs, and may be willing to purchase (at a premium) the specific products or services they desire from private companies. If there is a large enough market demand, service-based, for-profit counterparts of public benefit organizations might be launched to address those needs. These for-profit organizations will rank Customers much higher than their public counterparts.

Fed-Ex and UPS (Social-Physical) are prime examples of organizations that put Customers first, as opposed to the U.S. Postal Service. For-profit education companies and privately run healthcare facilities also differ from their Causal cousins (public schools/universities and government run clinics/hospitals). With many of these for-profit, Customer-oriented companies, you get what you pay for. Better products, more expertise and faster service often cost more. Although I would argue that many public institutions are inefficient and rank Employees and/or Customers too low, I believe that the disconnect between expectations and results are caused by both sides of the issue— We pay too little, expect to much, AND receive less than full value from these public organizations relative to our investment.

Charter schools have been an interesting development in (and wake-up call for) public education. In the case of my children's schools, this experiment has better aligned the needs/expectations of stakeholders and created significant value relative to their investments. The stronger voice of parents (through "funding votes") has positively impacted the learning experiences of our children. Fortunately, however, the administrators of our schools have been able to channel the energy and interest of caring parents and donors into creative projects that build value. Rather than allowing passionate parents to dominate their schools, school principals rally parental support to the benefit of their teachers (and students). These administrators recognize that they are managing

Causal Organizations and place their Employees (teachers) first, as it is them that should create the most value. However, by operating with small capital budgets, these organizations have also improved the ranking of their Customers (students and parents)—By renting facilities and equipment, the expectations and power of Shareholders (the government / taxpayers) are diminished. Attracting gifted teachers interested in developing their protégés in student-oriented environments supported by interested parents has not been difficult, despite modest salaries. As Employees, they crave Causal Organizations that have a defined purpose supported by aligned administrators, staff and parents.

*   *   *

EPILOGUE

FINAL COMMENTS

I am intellectually curious about organizations of all types. I enjoy leading, serving and building successful organizations. So it was exciting for me to develop this managerial tool.

¡POW! is a decision making framework that has helped me during many difficult assignments. Each time I apply it, I get more confident in its strengths. I am becoming better at classifying organizations and implementing effective resource allocations. But even I am learning about the power of *¡POW!*

Pathways to Organizational Wealth would benefit from a more rigorous study into its constructs (I wish I had the time!). I know the classification schemes work and have enjoyed guiding organizations along its pathways. But I would like to see more work done to improve this model. For example, this framework would benefit from a more objective method for classifying organizations. What objective measure could be utilized to determine whether an organization is Physical, Social or

Causal? Is there data currently collected that could help make this determination fast and simple? Does additional objective information exist that could help refine the classification of organizations into our six subgroups?

I have not been able to find simple answers to these questions yet. Perhaps my research block stems from my bias towards the communal approach to classification. I find significant value in debating the classification of an organization. This step allows for an interesting strategic discussion to take place. The debate requires defining the meaning of organizational wealth, prioritizing stakeholders, clarifying their needs and measuring their opinions.

As you have probably guessed, I enjoy interacting with this framework at work and during my leisure time. I find myself classifying businesses as I read about them in the paper or while driving past them in my car. For fun, I attempt to plot organizations based on articles or books that chronicle their successes. The resulting charts illustrate the power of this approach and the wealth created by enterprises exceeding the expectations of their primary stakeholders.

I hope that you will also enjoy applying, researching or debating this management framework. Thank you for considering these concepts. And good luck in leading your enterprise along its *Pathway to Organizational Wealth* and towards *Euphoria*!

OTHER

DEFINING *¡POWⅡSMS*—
GLOSSARY OF IMPORTANT TERMS

Acceptable :

Zone II on the chart. An *Acceptable* organization is operating in positive territory. All stakeholders feel better than Neutral about results, but no expectations are being met.

Causal Asset :

One of three core asset types leveraged by an organization to create value for stakeholders. Causal Assets can be based on such esoteric concepts as values, purpose, and/or beliefs that have an enormous impact on organizational productivity, creativity and wealth. Causal Assets can affect a person's life and an organization's development (and valuation) profoundly without necessarily having a direct link to profitability. They can be energizing, healing, rejuvenating and abundant. Examples might include the mission/purpose of the organization, its communal values, its collective norms, philosophies and beliefs.

Causal Organization :

An organization in which core, value-creating mechanisms are dominated by Causal Assets. These organizations are driven to make the world a better place by feeding, healing or counseling their Customers. Employees (including volunteers) create the most value in these organizations and often invest the most in them. Causal Organizations include everything from legal and social services for the disadvantaged to schools, hospitals and church organizations. The majority of Causal Organizations fall in the public benefit or not-for-profit categories as they are typically driven by something other than profits.

Customer :

A party that benefits from the products produced or services provided by an organization. Customers can include consumers, other businesses, patients, parishioners, and students.

Employee :

Any person that works with the organization to create the product or deliver the service that does not otherwise belong to a vendor or one of the other stakeholder groups. Employees can include volunteers, contracted agents, and temporary employees.

Euphoria :

Zone IV+, at the most positive apex on the chart. An organization operating in the state of *Euphoria* is exceeding the expectations of all stakeholders. It is abundant, energizing, and extremely valuable.

Inspirational :

Zone IV on the chart. An *Inspirational* organization is operating in very positive territory. It is meeting or exceeding the expectations of all primary stakeholders.

Not Tolerable :   A predominantly negative region on the chart. An organization that is Disappointing or Upsetting one or more stakeholders is *Not Tolerable.* Although this organization might be appeasing its primary stakeholder, the other stakeholders will apply pressure for improvement.

Organizational Classifications :

| | Stakeholder Ranking | | |
Organizational Type	First	Second	Third
Physical—Social	Shareholders	Customers	Employees
Physical—Causal	Shareholders	Employees	Customers
Social—Causal	Customers	Employees	Shareholders
Social—Physical	Customers	Shareholders	Employees
Causal—Social	Employees	Customers	Shareholders
Causal—Physical	Employees	Shareholders	Customers

Organizational Classifications—Examples:

Organizational Type	General Example	Specific Examples
Physical—Social	Manufacturer-Consumer Products	Procter & Gamble
Physical—Causal	Manufacturer-Technology	Genentech, Medtronic
Social—Causal	Consulting Services	Ad Agency, Law Firm
Social—Physical	Product Retailers	Nordstrom, Sears
Causal—Social	Not-for-Profit Services	Big Brother/ Big Sister
Causal—Physical	Public Benefit Organizations	Hospitals, Universities

Physical Asset: One of three core asset types leveraged by an organization to create value for stakeholders. Physical Assets have three important properties. First, a Physical Asset depreciates even when maintained. Second, it can only be utilized in one place at one time. This explicit physical scarcity can result in an associated opportunity cost when it is deployed. And third, a Physical Asset must typically generate more cash (or utility) than its cost of maintenance for its value to increase (holding risk factors, return expectations and replacement costs equal). Equipment, buildings and inventory fit easily into this category.

Physical Organization:

An organization in which core, value-creating mechanisms are dominated by Physical Assets. These organizations will typically require significant amounts of capital to fund their initial investments in buildings, equipment and inventory. Ongoing maintenance of these core assets will require significant reinvestments. Examples of Physical Organizations include manufacturing enterprises of all types.

¡POW!:   The most direct, efficient "*Pathway to Organizational Wealth*" that an organization of a particular type can take.

Purpose of an Organization:

To meet or exceed the expectations of wealth or value creation of its primary stakeholders by investing in and leveraging its core assets.

Shareholder: A party that has given financial capital to an organization. Shareholders can include investors, donors and sponsors.

Social Asset :

One of three core asset types leveraged by an organization to create value for stakeholders. Social Assets differ substantially from Physical Assets in two important ways. First, unlike its physical cousin, a Social Asset has the ability to appreciate when maintained. Second, a Social Asset can be leveraged in multiple ways simultaneously, it doesn't have physical limitations! Social Assets must increase in relevance or importance to its core stakeholders while maintaining or increasing their relative scarcity at the margin for their value to increase. There is also no definitive need for a pure Social Asset to generate positive cash flows for its value to increase. The value of a Social Asset is often subjective. Examples of Social Assets include brands, relationships, and know how.

Social Organization :

An organization in which core, value-creating mechanisms are dominated by Social Assets. In contrast with Physical Organizations, very Social enterprises have (and need) a relatively small amount of fixed overhead (i.e. Physical constructs). As a result, Social Organizations tend to be very scaleable. They have a relatively low need for initial and ongoing capital but have high current expenses like wages and advertising. The core assets invested in and leveraged by Social Organizations include Customer relationships and intellectual property like brands, trademarks, and patents. Service-based enterprises are classic Social Organizations.

Stakeholder :

A party that has an interest in or that could be impacted by an organization. Stakeholders include Employees, Customers, Shareholders, community members, government agencies, and protectors of the environment.

Start-up : An organization that was recently founded.

Temporarily Acceptable :
Zone I on the chart. A *Temporarily Acceptable* organization is operating in positive territory for its primary stakeholder, but mildly Disappointing other stakeholders. This situation is expected to improve within an acceptable timeframe.

Turn-around : A troubled organization that is in the process of being improved.

Unacceptable : The most negative region on the chart. An organization that is Disappointing or Upsetting all stakeholders is considered to be *Unacceptable*. Such an organization would be pressured to change quickly.

Valuable : Zone III on the chart. A *Valuable* organization is operating in positive territory for most, if not all, of its stakeholders, and meeting or exceeding the expectations of its most important stakeholder.

www.ingramcontent.com/pod-product-compliance
Lightning Source LLC
Chambersburg PA
CBHW022108170526
45157CB00004B/1532